Falconer on the Edge

Falconer on the Edge

A MAN, HIS BIRDS,
AND THE VANISHING LANDSCAPE
OF THE AMERICAN WEST

Rachel Dickinson

Houghton Mifflin Harcourt
BOSTON NEW YORK
2009

www.hmhbooks.com

Library of Congress Cataloging-in-Publication Data

Dickinson, Rachel.
  Falconer on the edge : a man, his birds, and the vanishing landscape of the American West / Rachel Dickinson.
     p. cm.
  ISBN-13: 978-0-618-80623-2
  ISBN-10: 0-618-80623-7
1. Chindgren, Steve. 2. Falconers—United States—Biography.
3. Falconry—West (U.S.) I. Title.
  SK17.C499D53 2009
  799.2'32092—dc22   2008050164

Book design by Anne Chalmers
Typefaces: Miller, Barbera

Printed in the United States of America

DOC 10 9 8 7 6 5 4 3 2 1

For Tim
and my children—
Railey, Clara, Jack, and Gwendolyn

Contents

Prologue

THIS STORY BEGINS the afternoon my husband brought home a kestrel—America's smallest falcon—in a paper bag. He carefully opened the top, and I peered in to see a pretty little bird hunkered down in the bottom of the sack. It had a rufous back and a dark slate blue cap on its cream-colored head. It turned slightly to look up at me, or maybe at the light, but it made no move to try to escape. Tim told me the young bird had been rescued by a woman in a trailer park who'd seen some boys trying to feed it a ham sandwich. She knew that that probably wasn't a good idea, so she got the bird into a bag and drove to Cornell's Lab of Ornithology, where the bag went from desk to desk until it got to Tim's. When I asked Tim why he'd kept the bird, it all came tumbling out—*I've got to get my license renewed and build a mews and get some food* . . . He stopped when he saw me looking at him as if he had suddenly grown an extra head.

"I have no idea what you're talking about," I said.

"I'm a falconer," he said. "I just haven't had a bird for about twelve years."

I met my husband, Tim Gallagher, when he came to town to take the job as editor of *Living Bird*, the flagship publication of the Cornell Lab of Ornithology. It was the fall of 1990, and

I was living with my five-year-old daughter in a little Sears house in the village of Freeville, about ten miles from Ithaca, New York. I grew up in Freeville, and the Sears house was one that I had always loved as a kid. I used to ride my Spyder Bike slowly past the house because I thought it looked like a cottage that might be found in the English countryside—everything I knew I got from the movies, so I was probably thinking of *The Enchanted Cottage* with Dorothy McGuire and Robert Young. In the first half of the twentieth century, you could mail-order a Sears house; all the pieces came by train and were then assembled on your lot. When it was new and in pieces, it had cost around a thousand dollars, but when I met Tim I had just purchased it for sixty times that—the going price for five rooms, a bathroom, and the potential for major cuteness.

My next-door neighbor worked at the Lab of Ornithology, and one day she told me she had a new boss and he was single. She invited both of us to her New Year's Eve party, and that was all it took. He introduced me to the world of birds, I introduced him to my daughter, and eight months later we were married by the village mayor.

Over the next couple of years, Tim and I learned a lot about each other, but for some reason he never told me he was a falconer, never told me about the sport that had probably been the most important thing in his life for decades. Tim was forty years old when I met him, and his falconry was so completely in remission that it never came up.

Once the cat—or, more accurately, the falcon—was out of the bag, I watched Tim throw himself into making plans for the kestrel. There's an avalanche of paperwork required to obtain a falconry permit, so it took quite a bit of time, energy, and ingenuity for Tim to once again become a master falconer. Initially, he became a subpermittee for a local wildlife rehabilitator so that he could legally work with the bird. For a while, the kestrel lived in a flight chamber at the old Peregrine Fund barn at Cornell, where researchers in the 1970s and '80s had bred thousands of young peregrine falcons and released them into the wild to reverse the population crash of the species.

I was amused by the whole project. The kestrel was such a feisty little thing—she made screeching noises when you got too near—and seemed fiercely devoted to Tim, calling sweetly whenever she saw him and fluttering her wings. Although at that point, I didn't really have an interest in falconry, I loved watching the little falcon move around in her enclosure. By this time we had a couple more kids and they also loved watching the little falcon. They dubbed her Strawberry, and the name stuck.

Throughout that summer and fall, during his lunch break Tim flew Strawberry in a small meadow near his office. His plan was to teach her to hunt and then release her back into the wild before winter. She'd fly over the field of tall grass and go after grasshoppers buzzing and flying among the stems, as well as mice and voles that ran on little paths through the field, and she caught quite a few of them. Tim called her in by blowing a whistle he wore around his neck, but there were times when she'd ignore him and land on the power line that ran through the middle of the field or on one of the fence posts that marked the boundaries of the meadow. Once perched, she would just sit and look at him.

The time finally arrived when Tim felt he could set Strawberry free, and he released her in a nearby field. All went well for several weeks. But then winter set in and life became difficult for the young falcon. We finally got a call from a local travel agent who said that his mother had trapped a small falcon that had been hanging around her back deck, shrieking and bothering the songbirds. She'd had no problem luring the kestrel into a birdcage; she put bits of meat on the bottom and then slammed the door when the bird went in to eat. When Tim went to pick up Strawberry, the woman asked if she could keep the bird. Tim told her it was against the law to own a raptor unless you were a licensed falconer but he assured her that he would take good care of the falcon. She watched silently as Tim opened the cage, picked up Strawberry, and carried her back to his Jeep.

Tim soon gave up any idea of releasing Strawberry. She was clearly too attached to people to be set free. Over the next few months, I learned a lot about falconry by watching Tim with his bird, although I kept the whole thing at arm's length. Maybe I thought that if I learned too much about the sport or about the birds, I'd have to take some kind of responsibility for them or, at the very least, be able to carry on an intelligent conversation about them. On the weekends, we managed to turn Tim's falconry into a family event. Tim would take the kestrel to the field near his office, and the kids and I would tag along, ostensibly so we could all watch Strawberry fly. While the kids ran around through the tall grass like puppies, Tim would walk to another part of the field with his little falcon riding on his gloved left hand. At some point Tim would stop walking, hold out his arm, and then, with a start, Strawberry would lift off his fist to fly after grasshoppers and mice.

The next thing I knew, Tim showed up with another falcon, a wild merlin that had been hit by a car and needed to be rehabilitated. So now we were taking two birds to the field. And then it happened: Tim got a call from an old friend, a falcon breeder in California, who had a young peregrine falcon he wanted to give to Tim. Not an orphan, not a rehab bird, but a perfect young falcon, ready to be trained as a hunter. I knew Tim had crossed an invisible line and was now becoming an obsessive, over-the-top falconer, as I suspected he had been in his teens and twenties. The bird was shipped to Ithaca from San Diego and arrived at the airport in a small dog carrier with all the windows blocked by black paper. The necessary transit documents were taped to the side, along with a big sign that said Do Not Open—Live Falcon. It caused quite a stir in the airport when it came out with the luggage.

A peregrine is *the* bird for anyone who wants to fly longwings. (*Longwing* is another word for falcon and presumably comes from the fact that the birds have long, tapered wings, particularly when compared with the shorter, more rounded wings of goshawks and Cooper's hawks, birds that falconers call shortwings.) Peregrines are spectacular flyers that ring up in the sky over the falconer and can reach heights of several thousand feet before they fold their wings to their sides and plunge toward earth and their prey. John James Audubon called them "great-footed hawks" because of their enormous feet and long, thin toes, which help them hit and then hold on to their prey. A peregrine is the size of a crow, a kestrel is blue-jay sized, and a merlin is between the two.

"These birds are not pets," Tim would insist. I know he meant that when he said it, but I would hear him giving little whistles at his peregrine Macduff as the bird ripped apart the dead quail that Tim had just given him. It didn't take me long to figure out that what I had thought of as a quaint, anachronistic hobby was now a full-blown obsession. Soon a big bag of frozen, day-old chicks—the male chicks that are culled from the local poultry farm—was crammed into the basement freezer. On a typical morning, I'd make a batch of waffles for the kids while Tim would take a few frozen yellow chicks, wrap them in paper towels, and defrost them in the microwave so they would be more lifelike in death when they were fed to the falcons.

By this time, Tim had built a mews in our attic. Our family had expanded, and we'd moved around the corner to a big pink Edwardian house that sat in the center of the village. There were dormer windows on three sides of the full attic, and Tim made enclosures around them to house the falcons. Strawberry often sat in the attic window that faced the front sidewalk. Sometimes as I went down the walk, I'd get a strange feeling, like I was being watched, and I'd turn around and see the falcon looking down at me.

During the falconry season, which in upstate New York lasts

through autumn and early winter, Tim gets up before dawn each day to take his peregrine to the field to get a flight in before work. He throws his waders in the back of the Jeep and loads up Macduff and the telemetry equipment (a battery-operated tracking device and receiver and antenna). He drives a circuit through the countryside, going past ponds he thinks might have ducks on them. When he finds one, he goes through an elaborate ritual of getting himself ready, getting the bird ready, releasing the bird in a field next to the pond, allowing it to circle high above him, then flushing the ducks from the pond by running at them and waving his arms like a wild man. Finally, he makes sure his bird doesn't get beat up by a thrashing duck if the peregrine happens to nail one.

During the falconry season, the birds sometimes get more of Tim's physical and emotional energies than his family does. It's like living with a sports nut—only Tim's sport includes the ultimate: death to the prey. There's a terrible and wonderful intensity that characterizes his devotion to falconry and to his birds. For years, there was a narrow distance between us that grew wider as the season progressed, and at times I felt myself losing ground to the peregrine in the fight for Tim's affections. As a nonfalconer, I found it hard to understand the fanaticism that comes with the years of dedication to this solitary pursuit. And ultimately, it is a solitary pursuit. You can be in the field with other falconers or with your family but in the end it comes down to the working relationship between you and your bird. It's the ultimate hunting partnership.

Tim hunts as if each day might be the last one of the hunting season. This is not an unreasonable assumption when you're hunting in upstate New York because in every falconry season there comes a morning when you wake up, look outside, and know all the good ponds will be frozen and empty of ducks. I think this feeling is also a function of Tim's age—he hunts as if each day might be his last day of hunting ever, as if each day might be the last time he will ever see his peregrine fly. This makes both the experience and the way he approaches everything during those months of hunting much more intense.

"Sweetest little wife, I think all the time of my little laughing, teasing beauty . . . and I could almost cry I love you so. But I think the hunting will do me good." On days in the midst of falconry season when I'm feeling kind and charitable, I think of these words written by Teddy Roosevelt and imagine that Tim has similar conflicted feelings. But there are times when he heads out the door at 5:30 or 6:00 A.M. to get a quick flight in before going to work when I want to say, *Enough already!* We've got three kids still at home, which means that for months I have to pull it all together myself to make sure they get breakfast, have their homework done, and catch the school bus on time.

Then a part of me frets a bit until Tim gets back home with the bird. If he's gone more than a couple of hours on the weekends or if I don't hear from him at work, I start to think he's lost his bird and is driving around the hills of the Finger Lakes holding a receiver out the window of the Jeep, trying to pick up a faint tracking signal from the transmitter attached to Macduff's leg. I also worry that maybe he stepped in a woodchuck hole and broke his ankle or had a heart attack as he ran toward a pond to try to flush ducks.

Maybe Homer was close to the truth when he wrote, "The hunter goes his way 'neath frigid skies, unmindful of his tender spouse." At night, in his dreams of spectacular flights of falcons and of powerful stoops at ducks, Tim also has images of real or imagined birds he's lost, and a feeling of overwhelming dread comes over him like a dark, suffocating blanket as he searches for something he will never find. He twitches and calls out in his sleep during hunting season. I think there's a place he goes, a place deep inside that I can't touch. It's primal. And it's exclusive.

Although I've accompanied him to the field to watch him fly his peregrine, and our conversations often include details about falconry as I ask questions and Tim gives patient answers, I didn't want to learn about flying a bird from my husband. I'm not sure exactly why. Maybe I didn't want to stress our easygoing relationship by casting myself in the student role and my husband as the teacher. Or maybe I didn't want to tap too deeply into that reservoir of Tim's that's filled not only with his vast knowledge of falconry but also with the complicated currents of his family and personal history.

Today Tim is a well-regarded editor, writer, and wildlife photographer. He's achieved a kind of legitimacy he never thought was possible when he was a young man. The common theme in his life—the thread that kept him tethered to responsibility—has always been falconry. It's the thing that made him get out of bed in the morning and kept him from wallowing in a drug-induced stupor during his late teens. Birds of prey need constant care, and Tim knew if he had birds he had to be responsible.

But I think falconry has always held a larger meaning for Tim. I suspect that as a young boy, Tim was able to find men he admired through falconry. Tim's father, Bill, had dragged the family halfway around the world—pulling Tim's mother and the kids away from her close-knit family in England—stopping in multiple places before they eventually wound up in Southern California. Bill Gallagher was a crackerjack salesman, and in each new place he'd always found a job in a department store. But eventually he would become bored and restless, and he'd move the family again. When they reached Southern California, via Malta and Toronto, he stopped uprooting the family and settled into drinking and terrorizing them when he got drunk. Having to care for and fly a bird meant Tim could escape the house and immerse himself in a world that required all of his attention.

I realized the depth of the connection between Tim and his birds when I saw him first with the kestrel, and then with the merlin, and finally with the peregrine. It went far beyond what you see when someone loves a cat or a dog. This working partnership between man and bird calls on all the senses when they are out in the field. It requires a falconer to have keen knowledge of the natural world: wind conditions, weather, where prey might be, the bird's temperament, and an understanding of the nuances of the bird's flight. The falconer also has to be in control of something that is ultimately uncontrollable. Once that bird is in the air, the falcon could leave and sever the relationship simply by flying away.

It struck me that to better understand this tumultuous love affair falconers have with their birds and their sport, I needed to take a step back from Tim. I thought if I could figure out what made a falconer tick—could figure out how a falconer gets up every morning during hunting season and manages to block out everything else in his life except the task at hand—maybe I could pull some universal truths from his story. And maybe these truths would help me better understand my husband and my relationship with him.

Over the years I'd read accounts of groups of falconers at grouse camps—gatherings of falconers who meet at different places in the West to fly their birds on sage grouse—so I decided to try to find a falconer to introduce me to this scene. Falconers who go to a grouse camp tend be the hardest of the hard core. They fly the biggest, fastest birds they can get, and they fly them at the most difficult upland game birds found in North America. They are maniacs about the sport. And as I learned about these falconers, one name kept popping up—Steve Chindgren.

So I picked up the phone and called him.

Falconer on the Edge

1

Hunting in Wyoming

I LEFT MY HOUSE in upstate New York on an October morning and felt the eyes of Tim's peregrine on me. Whenever I turned to the dormer window in the attic, he was always there, looking as if he would like to tear into my flesh. This is how falcons are: they're not social and they don't want to be your friend. They want to fly, to soar up and up until they're mere specks in the clouds looking down at the world beneath with their superenhanced vision. Did you know a falcon's eyeballs are so huge they take up most of its head and are separated from each other by only a thin membrane? So, yeah, I knew that bird wanted to rip into me, and because I'd anthropomorphized him, I assumed that he hated me because he was up there—trapped in a mews, looking through the vertical bars covering one section of the window where a pane of glass had been removed—and I was down here, on a sidewalk walking toward the post office, kicking the bronze-colored leaves that had fallen from the beech tree in the front yard.

A week later and halfway across the country, where the cool autumn wind blows through the sagebrush of the high desert in a desolate section of southwestern Wyoming, Steve Chindgren prepares his birds for the morning hunt. A small, wiry middle-

1

aged man, he has a great shock of reddish blond hair and a craggy, ruggedly handsome face with black-plastic-framed glasses perched on his small nose. Steve knows his birds love him. He knows they're not social birds, but he gave them life. People have had the ability to breed falcons in captivity only since the 1970s, and if this were evolution, the process would still be at the dinosaur stage. Steve flies hybrids, and breeding them isn't as simple as putting two birds in a room and leaving them to it. They are two different species, after all, and nature won't let anything happen—usually—unless people intervene and artificially inseminate the female with semen collected from the male.

A hybrid of a gyrfalcon (the world's largest falcon, which normally lives on the arctic tundra) and a peregrine (the poster bird for the Endangered Species Act in the United States and the only falcon that's found on seven continents) results in an *über*bird. The bird has stamina and speed and beauty. And Steve's creations love him like they'd love a mother. When they see him coming they keen and wail and *kak-kak-kak* because they know he will feed and care for them.

Steve flies several gyr-peregrine hybrid falcons every morning during the falconry season, which in Wyoming runs from September through February. This season he has his old bird Jomo, the bird he loves most in the world and a stunning hunting partner that's seen him into middle age; Jahanna, the bird he's pinning his hopes on to carry him well into old age; Tava, a young bird who's turning into an effective hunter; and Zaduke, a first-year bird that's he's training. When Steve heads out to the field in the morning before the hint of daybreak, the back of his truck is filled with falcons. They're hooded, to keep them calm, and tethered to perches made from two-by-eights turned on their sides, covered with AstroTurf, and bolted to heavy metal plates. And he always has a couple of English pointers in wooden dog boxes that are built snug against the cab of the silver Toyota Tundra.

Steve unhooks Jomo from his perch on the floor of the truck bed. Jomo, which means "hunter" in Swahili, earned his name long ago. He's the Hank Aaron, the Sammy Sosa, the Michael Jordan, the Tiger Woods of falcons. Because of Jomo's deadly prowess, an unbelievable number of sage grouse have been slammed into the ground, resulting in a shower of feathers that look quite beautiful as they float up and then back down to gently cover the bodies of the two birds—one dying on the ground and the other clinging to the warm flesh and guarding his kill with outstretched wings.

The sun is just peeking above the horizon, illuminating the desert floor with sharp rays of light like knife points, piercing the woody branches of the low-slung sagebrush at oblique angles. Miles and miles of sagebrush, more gray than green, surround the Toyota holding the falcons, the dogs, and the hunter. In the predawn light, the desert vegetation had looked soft, as if, if you could reach out and stroke it, it might tickle your hand. But the light shards of dawn show the plants for what they really are: Prickly. Sharp. A million hiding places for a chicken-sized bird.

Don't let their chicken size fool you. The sage grouse is the largest North American grouse; it weighs in at close to seven pounds, sometimes more, so it's about five times heavier than Jomo. You'd think it would fly like some goddamned Perdue bird, little tiny wings flapping and straining to move that mass off the ground, but you'd be mistaken. These birds are masterfully crafted, and when they take off—when they blow out of their deep cover and head for the nearest ridge—they look like large footballs with fast, whirring wings. They fly straight and hard and have the strength and stamina to go for miles across the desert, flying just feet above the desert floor and their beloved sagebrush—their food, their home, their security.

Steve scans the desert and doesn't see a thing moving except the sun, which steadily inches above the horizon. With

Jomo sitting on his gloved left fist, he picks up a long wooden pole from the truck bed, reaches past Jahanna, and pokes it toward the back of the truck, making contact with a metal plate that opens a spring latch on the English pointer's dog box. Out shoots Tucker, moving like a young thoroughbred at the starting gate of his first race. Steve knows he's coming and stands out of the way as the ginger-and-white dog blows past and hurls himself off the end of the tailgate.

"Tucker, find birds. *Find birds.*" And Tucker takes off running full out, nose in the air, ears flapping. The dog races back and forth in sweeping hundred-foot arcs in front of Steve. Suddenly he slows way down; his back gets straight as a board; his tail goes out; and he looks at a bush right in front of him. He begins to creep forward.

"Tucker, Tucker, *Tucker!*" The dog puts on the brakes at the sound of his name and looks back at Steve. *What the hell's your problem,* the dog's skin and bones and sinew and muscle body language seem to say. *"Tuckerwait!"* With his right hand and his teeth, Steve loosens the laces on the leather hood that covers all of Jomo's head except for his razor-sharp bill. With a fluid movement, Steve brings the hood forward and over the bird's head, and those enormous black eyes blink just once and then begin to take it all in—the dog, the desert, the sun, the sagebrush.

Jomo bobs his head up and down several times as he looks around. This is how a falcon triangulates. It uses motion parallax to determine distance, and its eyes, each of which has two foveae (the human eye has one), take in two images of a single object and allow the bird to see a true stereoscopic image and give depth perception to whatever it's looking at. What's also neat is that, like most birds, the falcon can look at objects in two different places—one in front and one to the side—and see them both simultaneously. Jim Enderson, a biologist and falconer, writes, "The view to the side is apparently seen more sharply, because falcons peer sideways at small, distant objects using one eye, but ahead with both eyes if the thing is near."

When he's done looking around, Jomo rouses—puffs his feathers out—then lets loose a stream of white crap. He pushes off Steve's gloved fist as his wings open and he takes off.

This takes all of thirty seconds.

As Steve watches Jomo work his way up to a good pitch with slow and deliberate wing beats, he can't help but think that he's also slowing down. At age fifty-six, he's in remarkably good shape and can outrun men half his age—a necessary skill if someone's going to hunt with birds and dogs in wide-open landscapes. He often says that the perfect joy of old age would be lying in bed and realizing that nothing hurts. Instead, every morning, Steve has to go through a whole ritual just to get himself moving. He says it feels as if every night someone injects plaster of Paris between the vertebrae in his lower back and by the time morning rolls around it's set hard as a rock. If he sneezes in the morning before he does his stretches, it causes excruciating pain. And if he's not really, really careful, his back goes out on him. Steve says he thinks the lining separating his vertebrae is so bad that at night his bones are starting to fuse together. He doesn't know if bones actually do that, but sometimes his back feels just awful, and as he watches his old bird fly, he's reminded of himself.

Jomo pumps his pointed wings faster and faster to climb higher into the ever brightening sky. Steve moves forward, keeping an eye on the dog and an eye on the bird. Actually, he has to turn his head at a funny angle to look for the bird because he is blind in one eye. The dog, the bird, the brightening sky—it's all happening at once, and Steve is like the puppet master pulling the strings. Steve knows those grouse are hunkered down under the sagebrush and aren't going to move unless they're about to get stepped on.

Tucker starts to creep forward again and then freezes, tail straight out, whole body quivering. "Whoa, Tucker, whoa, boy.

Whoa. Tucker. *Whoa."* The dog takes tiny steps forward, lining up on the birds, like a ballerina on pointe thinking about losing her balance. Steve, with his hand held out toward the dog as if to say *Don't even think about it,* cocks his head to look at Jomo, who's waiting on (that is, flying in tight circles) about a thousand feet over his head. It all has to align like a high school geometry equation. Then, as Jomo approaches Steve in his circle formation, Steve runs toward Tucker, whooping and hollering, and five grouse decide that the crazy man on the ground might be more dangerous than the deadly bird overhead. Those five grouse burst from the brush like forward passes thrown simultaneously but at slightly different trajectories at receivers racing toward the open end zone.

Ka-thump ka-thump ka-thump ka-thump. Steve's heart works overtime as he cocks his head to look up.

Jomo plummets earthward like a stone falling from a great height. Head down, wings folded to his sides; if you could slow that action and take a good look at what's going on during the power dive, you'd see his body elongating and becoming the perfect aerodynamic shape. Somehow he manages to choose one of the five grouse to aim at, and he flies toward the bird indirectly to better use his acute side vision. In the last moments before impact, Jomo shifts the angle and flies directly at the grouse, then hits it—*wham!*—like a pile driver.

The soft explosion of feathers falls like a dusting of early-winter snow on the predator and his prey. Disney might portray this whole scene as the circle of life, but this isn't a cartoon, and when we witness it, it pulls on some coded prehistoric gene that still remains from the time when we were hunters and killed because we had to. Steve runs toward the birds to watch the falcon cling to the body of the slain grouse and calmly rip hunks of bloody meat from the still warm breast.

Steve, who loves Jomo and knows that Jomo loves him, watches his bird eat for a minute, then offers Jomo a dead sparrow that he takes from his game bag. Jomo accepts the morsel because the taste of sparrow is his favorite thing. Steve kneels at the kill and rips out the guts of the sage grouse with his pocketknife, then throws them to Tucker, who's standing and watching nearby, waiting for his reward for a job well done.

He lets the dog enjoy his tidbit and the falcon eat his sparrow but is aware that the sun is well above the horizon now. He picks up the sage grouse carcass and puts it into his game bag. Later he'll marinate the breast meat for dinner and feed the rest of the grouse to his falcons. Steve's binoculars are hanging around his neck, and he brings them up to his eyes and looks around the desert, scanning the sky and then focusing on a low-slung ridge about a mile away. He thinks he saw some movement. Time to get the bird back into the truck. Time to move on to the next spot and away from the golden eagles that are starting to soar.

Some falconers refer to golden eagles as black dragons, an evocative name for the huge, dark, powerful birds that cast menacing shadows when they fly over the desert. They have very long, broad wings that span about seven feet. Opportunistic hunters, they'll go after anything they think they can catch and eat. A falcon down on a kill preoccupied by feeding is easy prey for an eagle. It'll watch a falcon that's hunting and wait for the chance to either snag the falcon or steal whatever it has just killed. Although eagles usually fly at about thirty miles an hour, they can reach speeds of up to a hundred miles an hour and can certainly outfly a falcon that's tired from hunting. Over the years Steve's had several birds killed by golden eagles, so you'd think he'd hate them, but he doesn't. He admires their speed and cunning and power. He knows that when they come in and kill one of his birds, they're just doing what they're supposed to be doing, and in some ways, when it happens, he has only himself to blame.

After a dinner of grilled marinated sage grouse, we started hitting the single-malt whiskey. Within an hour, we had moved from the dining room table to the living room, where we sat on the overstuffed leather couches. We raised our glasses to Jomo—a compact killing machine of a bird. It was his twentieth season of flying, and he consistently got his quarry, which was almost always a sage grouse that outweighed him by about fivefold. In fact, he'd made an average of more than fifty kills a season, which was simply phenomenal. No other falcon even came close; I know of one falconer who has spent about two dozen days hunting sage grouse in Wyoming over the past two years and hasn't gotten a single bird.

Compare the number of grouse caught by falcons in a year, probably not much more than a hundred, with the number of grouse that gun hunters kill in a single season in Wyoming, which is in the thousands. I can't even imagine what people mean when they say falconry has a negative impact on the sage grouse population.

That grouse dinner took place on a chilly late October evening in Steve's falconry lodge, what he calls "the cabin," located right outside of Eden, Wyoming. Steve stood near the pellet stove that had been wedged into a stone fireplace in the center of the large room. *Cabin* conjures up an image of lots of wood—which is correct—and of roughing it, which is not. The lodge is anything but rough, with its comfortable furniture, beautiful kitchen, and thick down quilts to burrow into while the Wyoming winds howl outside the windows. Steve lives near Salt Lake City but during the falconry season spends Monday through Friday at the cabin, returning home on the weekends to see his wife and two daughters.

A year earlier, Gary Boberg, a friend of Steve's and a fellow falconer, said, "Steve doesn't feel right if he hasn't killed something today." Boberg owns an air-conditioning business in Southern California. In a weird twist, Gary has known of Tim since he was a kid. Tim's sister Janet was in a ninth-grade art class with Gary, and one time she walked past his desk, looked down, saw a drawing he'd made, and said, "Nice Cooper's hawk." Gary was so shocked that anyone knew what the bird was that he talked to Janet and found out that her big brother was a falconer. Many, many years later, Gary sent the peregrine Macduff to Tim, out of friendship and because he wanted Tim to start flying birds again. Gary and Steve have also been friends for years because the western falconry community is pretty tight, and even though they live a couple of states apart, they visit each other regularly to hunt.

Steve didn't dispute Gary's characterization of his lust for blood. He couldn't understand why anyone would have a powerful hunting partner like a falcon and not be out in the field hawking for game every possible moment. As a way of explaining his intense attraction to falconry, that night he began to tell me stories of his childhood, of growing up in Emigration Canyon on the outskirts of Salt Lake City in the 1950s.

When he was a kid, Steve loved anything that moved—still does. He collected scorpions from the canyon when he was eight or nine and set up a stand in front of the house with a sign advertising: Scorpions for Sale—35¢ Live, 45¢ Pickled. Pretty soon some graduate students from the university who used scorpions in their research heard that Steve was selling scorpions, and they bought some from him and tried to get him to reveal his source. "Where are you getting these from, kid?" they asked, and Steve coyly replied, "Scorpion Town." He knew, even though he was a kid, that if he gave up the location, these guys would bypass him and get their own scorpions.

He talked about his early interest in dinosaurs and how he used to copy pictures of dinosaurs into a sketchbook and how one day he saw a Cooper's hawk in the backyard and was stunned by its fierce look and bright red eye. He ran to his sketchbook and found the picture he'd drawn of the *Tyrannosaurus rex*. He erased the dinosaur's mouth and drew in a beak and then just stared at the picture because it reminded him so much of the Cooper's hawk. He talked about his first red-tail, Shoulders, and how she got lost once and then showed up on Christmas morning. Steve paused in the story and refilled his glass with scotch.

"I knew it was a miracle," he said as he took another sip.

He talked about what it was like living in the Scamp, a travel trailer that year after year he parked on a wide spot of the Little Sandy River during the hunting season, and how grateful he was to have the cabin now. He looked around with bleary eyes and took in the artwork and the taxidermied sage grouse and the lovely furniture. Then he pointed to the back and through the kitchen window, and deep in the dark October night I could just barely see the outline of an old trailer—the kind that'd get pulled behind a beater car. It was such a teeny-tiny trailer that I couldn't believe it'd hold more than one or maybe—maybe— two people. It was the Scamp. I tried to imagine living in that thing for months at a time, doing all the cooking on a Coleman stove and then washing the dishes in the river. "I got my heat from a propane heater that sounded like a blowtorch when you turned it on," Steve remembered. "At night it became a tossup between freezing and being kept awake by the noise."

Steve joked that when Jomo died he'd like to put the bird's body in the Scamp, tow it down to the riverbed, and then light the whole thing on fire. "It'd be a proper Viking funeral for both of them," he said, and all you had to do was look at his face to see that he was actually serious.

The following morning when we bounced along in the pre-dawn on our way to the first flying field, Steve told me he was expecting a number of guests later that day. Kevin, a friend of Steve's since high school, had asked if he could come to the cabin, and Steve had said yes because he hadn't seen Kevin in a while now that he no longer lived in Salt Lake City. Then Kevin had asked if his father could come. "No problem," said Steve.

Then Kevin said his brothers had heard about the trip and wanted to come along. So later that day Steve expected the four of them, and he was kicking himself for saying yes. (As it turned out, they were really fun and helped out around the place, taking some of the pressure off Steve.) Later in the week Steve was hosting the annual grouse camp banquet at the cabin—an evening when fifteen or twenty falconers show up, drink a lot, eat a lot of food, and tell tall tales. He loved the annual dinner but was already feeling stressed about it.

"I need a vacation," he said. "I'm not going to let this happen next year. It's my own damn fault. I tell people that I'm not here on the weekends and they say, 'Well, we're going to be there Saturday and Sunday,' and because the rest of the world has the weekends off they build those days into their vacation. I tell people to try and plan their trips between Monday and Friday but no one does, and that just leaves me up here constantly, never getting a break. I swear I'm not going to do it next year. I'm going to say, If you want to be here Saturday and Sunday, you're going to have to get a motel because I'm not going to be here. That would be terrific. This is really hard on my wife because I don't get home on weekends and it's hard on me as well." We rode along in silence for a few more minutes and then Steve muttered, "I'm just too nice."

It was hard on Steve, but he'd put himself in this bind. His friend Joe Harmer, who lives down the road in Farson, told me that Steve's always saying he's going to tell people when they come up they have to take care of themselves. "He was so furious last year but he doesn't tell people that he's furious. The phone will ring and on the final ring, he'll pick it up and say, 'Hi, oh, how ya been?' And next thing you know he's saying, 'Why don't you come up here?' And when he gets off the phone I say, 'Why you saying that?'"

Joe's lived in Farson since 2001 and he doesn't let anyone come stay with him. He lives in an old trailer that has tires piled on the roof to keep it from blowing away during a Wyoming windstorm. Joe's a slight man in his seventies with thick glasses and wispy gray hair that's always covered by a cap. He's good company and will never refuse the offer to come over for a cup of coffee in the cabin. It's best to stay away from certain topics, like politics, and though he constantly baits me with remarks about New York Democrats, I just laugh and change the subject. Joe's been flying birds since the late 1960s. When he saw his first falconer, Joe was in his late twenties, and after that he was completely hooked. He was a machinist in the Philadelphia area and owned his own shop for years. When he retired from the business, he moved to be where the good hawking was. Before that, he'd been coming to Farson to hawk for years, staying in the little motel in town with his bird and his dog. He loves living in Wyoming full-time. When Steve's in Salt Lake City, Joe checks on his cabin and the pigeons every couple of days.

Steve loves the cabin. He spent so many years camping on the bank of the creek in the little Scamp that he still pinches himself when he comes to the cabin because it's just so beautiful. And he loves to show off his birds and take people to fabulous hunting grounds. So Steve finds himself in a war between his ego and his desire for a bit of privacy, and his ego always wins. But not without a price. The cabin is on a septic system and draws water from a well, and when there's a houseful of guests, he can't do much laundry. The water also has a purification system—when it's on, it recycles the water, which fills up the septic system; when it's off, the water smells like sulfur. Steve has to remember to go into the basement at night and unplug the purification system so it doesn't keep running. Then there's the problem of people who visit and act like they're on vacation—they don't bring groceries and they forget how to cook and clean and expect Steve to pull it all together. This really pisses him off, but that doesn't stop him from doing everything anyway.

At the end of October, the hunting areas around Eden and Farson are overrun with falconers—you can't throw a stone without hitting one. There are groups of falconers who come in from different states and set up camps of Airstreams and RVs and, occasionally, tepees and tents. They bring their dogs and birds, and they're all in the area for one thing—to hunt sage grouse. Steve says there are a certain number of falconers who camp in the area now, and the regulars frown on new falconers because they start to get in one another's way. "Falconry takes so much space," he said. "Your bird's way up in the air, and if someone begins to swing a lure over a mile away, your bird will go over to them. Gun hunters can walk wherever they want, but a falcon commands the sky so you need a lot of space away from other falconers."

Falconers can be very possessive of their hunting fields, and although Steve hunts on public land, the people who set up grouse camps in the region know which areas are traditionally Steve's. Steve had gotten in touch with the falconers who'd be gathering that week so he'd know where they intended to hunt and could stay out of their way. They'd only be there for a week so it wasn't a huge disruption to Steve's schedule. He'd hunt those places until they got there, and then he'd make himself scarce for the week.

If you took a map of southwestern Wyoming and drew a circle forty miles in diameter with the cabin at the center, it would encompass most of Steve's hunting fields. Sometimes he goes even farther—up toward the Wind River Range or Pinedale—but that forty-mile circle is what he considers his home territory. And he always hawks on public land because he'd rather not deal with a private landowner, especially when there are tens of thousands of acres of sagebrush desert at his disposal.

I was at the cabin for that annual grouse camp banquet and met at least five Steves, three Daves, a couple Joes, and a number of other falconers from Texas, Wyoming, Utah, Nebraska, and California. Dinner was a rollicking affair with steaks, grilled marinated grouse, rice, and salad. And of course there was beer, wine, and lots of whiskey. It seemed like everyone had brought a bottle of whiskey, and we tried to drink it all up that night. At dinner the conversations ranged widely from falconry to politics and then back to hilarious stories of mishaps in the field. Steve drifted off to his room fairly early after he'd pounded down the whiskies for a couple of hours. At the end of the evening, I found myself at the table with two very drunk falconers from England who had heard about grouse camp and snagged an invitation to visit for a few days. As the evening wore on, and they had more to drink, their accents and what they were saying went from fairly understandable to absolutely mysterious. I finally got them into the basement bunkhouse without either one pitching headfirst down the treacherous stairs. Then I went back to the kitchen to make sure everything was in order and to enjoy a few moments of late-night quiet in the cabin. I tidied up a bit, knowing that Steve would be awake in just a few hours, bleary-eyed but ready to start another day of hawking.

2

History of Falconry

To UNDERSTAND FALCONRY—the art of hunting with a trained bird of prey—we have to look back into the past. We have to consider the origins of this archaic sport in order to place what Tim and Steve do in context. Seeing a falconer in the field looks anachronistic—as if you're watching something that could have happened hundreds or even thousands of years ago. It feels out of our time, yet oddly timeless.

Dipping into the history of falconry is like playing an ancient variation of the childhood game of telephone: the narratives are filled with hyperbole and exaggeration and weird impressions that get passed on and, in the retelling, changed so much that you come away thinking, *Now, how does that go?*

I can't really determine what's true and what's false, and I don't have the wherewithal to travel around the world to check the obscure little references. I think I'd also have to learn Middle English. I'm sure that there are a handful of people out there who will be very quick to point out where my version of the history of falconry goes astray, but in the meantime, Gentle Reader, I'm going to give you my impressionistic version of the history of the archaic sport so as to provide some context for today's American longwingers.

Falconry is a loose term—it refers to flying any kind of raptor or bird of prey. A raptor is a bird that comes from the order Falconiformes, family Accipitridae. These birds have large curved beaks and powerful feet, and are incredible flyers. Their eyes work like binoculars and they can zero in on their targets from great distances, which is a helpful quality to have when hunting a thousand feet above the ground. The two common classes of raptors used in falconry are falcons and hawks, but that doesn't mean you won't find people flying everything from eagles to owls to vultures (although the last group can't be taught to hunt since they're strictly carrion eaters and will go after dead things only). The term *hawking* is used by falconers to describe what they do, as in *Tomorrow morning I'm going to go hawking.*

But where does falconry come from? Why would anyone even think about forming a relationship with a bird that would just as soon take a chunk out of his arm or stick a taloned foot in his face as look at him? This is a complicated question that doesn't have a simple answer. Falconry probably developed early on when someone watched a falcon stoop on a duck and kill it and then thought, *Now, how can I make that work for me?* At some point, someone trapped a bird and figured out how to entice it to be a hunting partner to help put food on the table. Today, the reason people fly birds is less obvious. Some falconers are interested in the hunt only and keep careful track of the number of kills a bird makes each season. Others fly birds because they like to feel that they have a certain amount of control over—or ownership of—the sheer beauty of the flight of a bird of prey. Then there are the falconers like Steve and Tim who develop such deep, passionate responses to caring for and flying birds that they can't even imagine not being falconers. To them it's more than the thrill they get from the hunt or from seeing an amazing flight—falconry completely defines who they are, and if you took that away, well, I don't know what would happen. (Although, as I saw with Tim, it can go into a complete remission, but it's an opportunistic passion that lies in wait.)

This is an exotic sport, and its exoticism and human curiosity suck the rest of us in. What we find when we look closely at falconry is a finely tuned symbiotic relationship between man and a (somewhat) wild bird. The bird comes to rely on the falconer as the source of food—a perfect example is the peregrine that waits on, or flies in high, tight circles over, the falconer who's responsible for flushing game. And as outsiders looking in, we're intrigued by the slender thread of trust—trust that the falconer will provide food—that draws the bird back to the earthbound falconer, who looks like a maniac as he rushes through a field trying to kick up grouse or prairie chickens or as he throws rocks into a pond to flush ducks. If we think about it, we realize there's really nothing but this invisible tether that keeps the falcon from flying away.

From very early times, trained birds of prey were considered extremely valuable assets. Powerful white gyrfalcons were trapped in places like Norway and Iceland and then carried to other parts of Europe, where they were used as peace offerings and for ransoms—a king's ransom, as it were. History is riddled with instances of ransoms, fines, and rents being paid wholly or in part with hawks. In the reign of Edward III, the theft of a trained bird was punishable by death. A statute of Henry VII decreed that anyone convicted of stealing a hawk from a nest on another man's property would be imprisoned for a year and a day.

Depending on what you read and who you believe, the history of falconry may go back as far as 3,500 years. There are some carvings in Turkey that show a large bird sitting on the fist of a hunter who holds up a hare by its hind legs. About seven hundred years later, a small hawk with jesses—leather straps falconers place around the ankles of their birds—shows up in a bas-relief in northern Iraq. Who knows? These might be religious or symbolic carvings, or they might mean that falconry existed by the eighth century B.C. in the Middle East.

Zooarchaeologists—archaeologists who study the fossilized bones of mammals and birds—have discovered the bones of raptors at archaeological digs in the Middle East that go back eight to ten thousand years. It may be that falconry existed that long ago, or it may be that these bird bones were the remnants of dinner. It's hard to tell what's going on from a pile of bones, but it's an intriguing idea.

There are records of falconry from the Hunan Province in China from the seventh century B.C., and we know that trained goshawks were introduced to Japan from China around A.D. 300. Trained raptors and Asian falconers made their way west along the Silk Road with other valued goods like salt and silk, ultimately carrying falconry into the heart of Europe. Along the way, as falconers and their birds traveled through the steppes of Central Asia, the Mongols and the Scythians of southern Russia picked up the sport.

The Mongols spread falconry to the Persians, who most likely taught it to the Arabs. By the seventh century—the time of the prophet Muhammad—hawking was well established in Arabia. As Islam swept through Europe, so did falconry.

Genghis Khan, the twelfth-century Mongol ruler, considered hunting a kind of training ground for war and had regiments of hunters organized. Falconry was overseen by the ministry of war, and falconers found themselves in the ranks as bodyguards to Genghis Khan. Messengers of Genghis Khan, who traveled to the far reaches of his empire, carried with them the symbol of a gold falcon.

His grandson Kublai Khan conquered China and relocated the Mongol capital to Beijing. Like Genghis, the grandson believed in hunting on a grand scale. Marco Polo, the thirteenth-century Venetian with a serious case of wanderlust, traveled the Silk Road in search of adventure and stayed with and worked for Kublai Khan for a dozen years. Later, when Polo was imprisoned in Genoa, he related his travels to a fellow prisoner, who wrote down the stories. They were published as *Il Milione* and then translated as *The Travels of Marco Polo*. In this book, Polo said that Kublai Khan hunted from a palanquin carried by four elephants and lined with beaten gold. And Marco Polo said that on hunting expeditions Kublai Khan "takes with him full 10,000 falconers and some 500 gerfalcons, besides peregrines, sakers, and other hawks in great numbers, and goshawks able to fly at the water-fowl . . ." This could be the result of fanciful storytelling on Marco Polo's part, although other reports in the book that were initially dismissed as hogwash were later found to be true.

For some reason, hawking never caught on in Greece and was therefore slow to reach the Romans, who liked to emulate all things Grecian. The Romans were exposed to falconry late in their history when Julius Caesar conquered the Gauls in northern Europe and then pushed on into Britain.

Falconry was never practiced by Native Americans, and hawking never moved farther into the African continent than North Africa. And there is no actual evidence that the ancient Egyptians ever practiced the sport, although they did deify falcons, as seen by the thousands of little mummified bird bodies that show up in their tombs. And it seems that falconry has never been practiced by aboriginal people anywhere.

Hawking had certainly reached England by the seventh century. Ethelbert II, Saxon king of Kent, begged Archbishop Boniface for "two falcons of such skill and courage as readily to fly at and seize cranes and bring them to the ground." Alfred the Great, the ninth-century king of Wessex, was a falconer, and the beautiful Bayeux tapestry shows King Harold taking a trained raptor and hounds on his visit to William of Normandy in 1064.

The language of falconry comes from the Norman times in England. Words such as *eyas* and *lure* and *mews* come directly from Norman French. Even the word *falcon* is French based.

Falconry's big break came in the thirteenth century. Holy Roman emperor Frederick II of Hohenstaufen, a crusader, a scholar, and at various times king of Sicily and king of Jerusalem, was an avid falconer. A Renaissance man well before the Renaissance, Frederick was extremely curious about the world he lived in and surrounded himself with scholars—including Arabic scholars—who traveled with him from castle to castle as he engaged in relentless military campaigns to keep his vast landholdings intact. Frederick spent forty years writing his treatise *De Arte Venandi cum Avibus* (On the Art of Hunting with Birds), which was translated into English in 1943 and renamed *The Art of Falconry*. This book brought the world of medieval falconry to life for curious American falconers. Remarkably, many of Frederick's training techniques are practiced by falconers today.

The Middle Ages is surely the time period we all imagine when we think about falconry. It's easy to conjure up medieval hunting scenes complete with lords and ladies on horseback riding to hounds with birds in the air above them.

One of my favorite parts of falconry history is the list of who was allowed to do what in the highly regimented world of medieval falconry. It comes from *The Boke of St. Albans,* also called *The Book of Haukyng and Fyshyng,* written by Dame Juliana Berners, abbess of Sopwell, and printed in 1486. (It was the first British book to be printed in color.) She writes about hawking and hunting and fishing and heraldry and at one point sets forth the protocol for who was permitted to fly which bird. Who knows if this list reflects reality or not—it could have been a way to illustrate that the natural and social hierarchy was organized similarly in both hunting birds and humans. What this list does show is that there was a hierarchy in falconry, with the fastest, sleekest, sexiest birds at the top.

Ther is a Gerfawken. A Tercell of gerfauken. And theys belong
    to a Kyng.
Ther is a Fawken gentill, and a Tercell gentill, and theys be for
    a prynce.
Ther is a Fawken of the rock. And that is for a duke.
Ther is a Fawken peregrine. And that is for an Erle.
Also ther is a Bastarde and that hawk is for a Baron.
Ther is a Sacre and a Sacret. And theis be for a Knyght.
Ther is a Lanare and a Lanrett. And theys belong to a Squyer.
Ther is a Merlyon. And that hawke is for a lady.

The list goes on to say that a yeoman could use the goshawk
or hobby, which was said to be able to "sufficiently stock a lar-
der." Priests and holy water clerks flew the female and male
sparrow hawks respectively, and knaves, servants, and children
used the kestrel—the smallest falcon.

Most nobility didn't train their birds themselves. Instead,
they hired falconers. Master falconers were well paid to work
for kings and other nobles. The office of master of the mews
was created for the individual in charge of obtaining, grooming,
and keeping the king's best hawks in a constant state of readiness for hunting. Falconry terms start to appear in art and literature from about this time period—the works of Shakespeare
are rife with images drawn from falconry. I always think of the
scene from *The Taming of the Shrew* in which Petruchio talks
about taming Kate (act 4, scene 1):

> My falcon now is sharp and passing empty,
> And till she stoop she, must not be full-gorg'd,
> For then she never looks upon her lure.
> Another way I have to man my haggard,
> To make her come, and know her keeper's call,
> That is, to watch her, as we watch these kites
> That bate and beat and will not be obedient.

> She eats no meat to-day, nor none shall eat;
> Last night she slept not, nor to-night she shall not.

During the nineteenth century, interest in falconry in Britain decreased dramatically. There isn't any one thing you could point to that screams *That's why people aren't hunting with birds anymore!*; it was rather a combination of factors. The development of more accurate sporting guns meant that gentlemen could step out into the fields with their hounds and beaters and blow away hundreds of game birds in a day. Compare this with the work involved in flying a bird and the relatively miserable return in terms of dead game birds. With the industrial revolution in full swing, workers spent far more time in the factories and far less time in the fields scaring up food. Reigning monarchs in the nineteenth century were less interested in falconry (Queen Victoria probably didn't fly birds). But it was the passage of the Enclosure Acts of the late eighteenth and early nineteenth centuries that really sealed the deal.

Practicing falconry, particularly flying peregrines, demands a lot of space. The Enclosure Acts—and there were hundreds of them—consolidated and enclosed land throughout England that had once been used by everyone, from the lords to the peasants. All the good hawking country was now divided into a series of estates that were ringed by sturdy stone walls. This all but put an end to the gentlemanly sport of heron hawking, which required the use of horses to cover miles as falcons pursued herons through the sky. Small farmers and tenants had once been able to forage and hunt on land owned by large landholders, but they were now discouraged from doing so by gamekeepers who patrolled the grounds to keep the wildlife in and the riffraff out.

With the development of more accurate guns and the rise in sport hunting, a new threat to the peregrine emerged. Large estates often employed gamekeepers to manage and maintain populations of wild game birds. Peregrines—whose natural quarry includes game birds like red grouse—went from being the hunting partners of noblemen to competing with noblemen for the same quarry. Gamekeepers routinely shot adult peregrines and climbed to peregrine nests to smash eggs and kill the young in an effort to rid the area of falcons. This wholesale slaughter of peregrines occurred throughout much of Britain well into the twentieth century.

Not everyone, however, wished to see falconry abandoned. Falconry became almost strictly the purview of the elite, and falconry clubs were formed, such as the Loo Hawking Club in Holland (established in 1838), which catered to the European aristocracy. This club was succeeded by the Old Hawking Club of England, which employed professional falconers. Common people completely lost touch with the traditions and rituals surrounding falconry.

It's not surprising that falconry didn't make its way across the Atlantic to North America in the eighteenth and nineteenth centuries. Why would it? The men who were immigrating weren't the European elite—the ones who were keeping the falconry tradition alive—so that connective thread to the medieval sport never stretched across the ocean. But it's hard to believe that no one ever looked around and noticed the amazing raptors on the North American continent. Everywhere people looked they would have seen birds of prey hunting—depending on the part of the country, there'd be red-tails crashing through the woods after squirrels or dropping from branches onto bunnies; peregrines folding their wings to their sides and stooping on ducks; sharp-shins and Cooper's hawks pursuing small birds; ferruginous hawks and prairie falcons taking ground squirrels; or golden eagles going after anything that moved.

But falconry took time. Americans were busy driving west, clearing forests, killing bison, plowing up the prairie, and pushing the Indians farther and farther from their traditional lands.

They were creating towns and developing industries and engaging in nation-building. All of this took time and energy, and few hours in the day were left for leisure activities. Falconry took a lot of commitment—birds needed to be trapped and then cared for and trained. And no one but a person who was passionate about flying birds could take the time to make it happen. Additionally, only those who knew about falconry would attempt it.

Finally, those pioneers and settlers who even noticed birds of prey most likely viewed them as pests, much as they viewed wolves, coyotes, bears, and foxes. Some species of raptor were hazards to barnyard chickens, and pioneers took little time to distinguish among the various species. To them, they were all big chicken killers, and bounties, some of which were offered until the 1960s, were often given for the raptors' destruction. Places that we now think of as premier hawk-watching spots in North America—such as Hawk Mountain, Pennsylvania, and Cape May, New Jersey—were once the scenes of annual slaughters of hawks, falcons, and eagles as shotgun-wielding locals lined up shoulder to shoulder and blasted them out of the sky as they flew by in migration. Some shot the raptors for bounty, but many shot them just because they could.

It took the twentieth century and a confluence of factors before falconry took hold in the United States. In 1920, famed bird artist Louis Agassiz Fuertes illustrated an article about falconry entitled "Falconry, the Sport of Kings" for *National Geographic* magazine. In the 1930s the same magazine ran a few more articles by twin brothers Frank and John Craighead about flying birds and then hawking with an Indian prince. Every single hard-core falconer I've ever met mentions seeing these articles as a kid.

During the 1940s and 1950s, several men, including Colonel "Luff" Meredith (considered by many to be the father of American falconry), Al Nye, "Doc" Stabler, and Frank and John Craighead, got serious about falconry. They formed the Falconers'

Association of North America, which was short-lived because America got involved in World War II. But by the late 1950s, falconers in California had started to organize, and clubs like the Falconry Club of Southern California and, a bit later, the California Hawking Club were formed.

In 1961 the North American Falconers' Association (NAFA) was founded by a small group of falconers and became the official organization representing North American falconers. In the early 1970s, members of NAFA worked with the federal government to craft the first federal falconry laws. The United States has some of the most restrictive falconry legislation in the world, and its primary objective is to protect the birds of prey—not the falconers. Today there are a number of laws regulating American falconry, including portions of the International Convention for the Protection of Migratory Birds (1916), the Migratory Bird Treaty Act (1976 and 1981), the 1973 Convention on International Trade in Endangered Species of Wild Fauna and Flora (CITES), the Endangered Species Act (1976 and 1981), and the Wild Bird Conservation Act (1992).

Interest in falconry has exploded over the past couple of decades. Organizations like NAFA and state falconry clubs keep falconers connected through journals and newsletters and provide venues—falconry meets—for experienced falconers to gather and hunt together.

I think there are three things that have really jump-started falconry in the last twenty years: the peregrine falcon's return from the brink of extinction; our ability to create hybrid falcons; and the availability of Harris's hawks. Once threatened with extinction as a result of the effects of the pesticide DDT, the peregrine has been aggressively recovered through a program of captive breeding and hacking (that is, releasing the young birds into the wild) begun by falconers and the Peregrine Fund. The subspecies of peregrine originally found on the East Coast became extinct, but through the efforts of the

Peregrine Fund, peregrines of different subspecies—including *anatum, tundrius, pealei,* and even Spanish peregrines—have been introduced to the East, and these magnificent birds can now be found in historic nesting sites east of the Mississippi. Peregrines have also adapted well to urban life, where they can find a lot of food, mainly pigeons. Several cities have installed nest webcams, which give people ringside seats to the activities of peregrines nesting on the window ledges of tall buildings.

The federal government has issued four hundred breeding permits, and a falconer can now buy a captive-bred bird that's generations away from knowing about the hardships of surviving in the wild, especially during that first year, when as many as nine out of ten birds of prey perish. And the interbreeding of some falcon species has created superbirds—such as the gyrfalcon-peregrine crosses—that often have the best qualities of both parents. These super- or *über*birds and the availability of captive-bred gyrfalcons make hawking for big difficult prey possible.

Finally, the Harris's hawk—a beautiful large hawk traditionally found in the Southwest—has become extremely popular as a falconry bird. Unlike most raptors, Harris's hawks are social birds and often hang around in groups and hunt together. In captivity, they become like pets to many hawkers and will follow them in the field like aerial puppy dogs as they hunt mammals such as rabbits and squirrels.

Falconers were once a fairly secretive lot in America. They didn't want to call attention to themselves or their birds. In California in the early 1960s, Tim and his friends often trespassed on private property to fly their birds. They'd head out onto big tracts of land that belonged to absentee landowners who wouldn't have given them permission to fly the birds there for fear of lawsuits. But once the federal regulations were put into place, falconers risked having their birds confiscated and their falconry permits suspended if they were caught trespassing on private property or flying their birds at game that was out of season. Today, like Steve, many hard-core falconers fly their birds on public lands only, where they don't have to bother getting permission.

Now there are programs such as the British School of Falconry at the Equinox Hotel in Vermont and the nonflying public can take a peek into the mysterious world of falconry at places like SeaWorld and Renaissance fairs. For almost thirty years, Steve has done bird shows—first at the Tracy Aviary in Salt Lake City, then at the Hogle Zoo—and one of his goals is to wow the audience with the free flights of raptors.

When American falconers were first defining and learning their sport, in the mid-twentieth century, they turned to classic texts—like the thirteenth-century work by Frederick II—to learn about training their birds. Falconers embraced the archaic language of the sport as well as many of the traditional training methods. Being with a falconer is a bit like being with a foreigner whose language you don't speak. They talk about things like the *tiercel* (a male peregrine) and a *haggard* (an adult bird that's been trapped). The equipment used for the sport is called, collectively, the *furniture*. A bird might be *intermewed* (has gone through a molt while in captivity) or *hard-penned* (a young bird whose feathers are fully grown out and hardened) or a *brancher* (a very young bird that can scramble out of the nest but is not yet able to fly). To *cast off* a bird (release it from the fist) is not to be confused with *casting*, which is a pellet of indigestible materials like fur, bones, and feathers that's regurgitated by a raptor. The bells affixed to a hawk's ankles are secured to jesses by *bewits*. And once an *eyas* (a bird removed from the nest or *eyrie*), always an *eyas*. When I hear my husband using the word *callow* I don't assume he's talking about me or the children but rather about a nestling raptor.

When people hear that Tim's a falconer, they often ask how

he trains the bird to retrieve. The fact is, birds of prey don't retrieve. They hunt, and wherever the prey falls is where you're going to find your bird. Training your bird is a complex and never-ending process because conditions outside your control constantly change—one day there might be ducks on the pond, the next day none; a housing development might spring up on land that had been your favorite hawking field.

There are a couple of ways to acquire a bird. One is to go to a breeder, in which case the bird will be an eyas—a bird removed from a nest or the care of its parents. Another way a licensed falconer can get a bird is to trap one. A beginning falconer—an apprentice—has to trap a bird to use as his or her first falconry bird. The kinds of birds the falconer is allowed to trap vary slightly by state, but most first birds are red-tailed hawks or kestrels. Trapping is usually done during migration—the falconry regulations for each state give a time frame during which this is allowed—and apprentices can trap and train only first-year birds.

A bird that is first handled at a very young age imprints easily on the falconer and comes to view him or her as a parent or a mate, which adds a twist to the man-bird relationship. Traditional training methods call for leaving birds hooded, or in dark rooms, for great lengths of time to keep them calm. But the advent of captive-bred eyases has led to new approaches. Now chicks are often given the run of the house and kept close to humans as much as possible. This dispels the chicks' notion that every time they see a human they will be fed. It also deepens the bond between falconer and bird.

One of the first things a falconer does is get the bird used to a hood—an intricately crafted leather headpiece that covers all of the bird's head except for its beak. Once hooded, the bird is calm because it's dark. A hood often has a leather or feather topknot, which gives the falcon a truly exotic look. The bird is hooded while it's standing on the falconer's fist—for a European or an American, it's always the left fist, unless the falconer is left-handed. With his right hand, the falconer puts the hood on the bird in one swift motion, and he is able to take it off just as quickly. He tightens the hood by pulling on one strap, or brace, with his right hand and pulling on the other brace with his teeth. The bird's cooperation with being hooded can be wrecked by someone who is hesitant or not good at hooding the bird. This can affect the entire bird-man relationship. The hood allows the bird to be transported without freaking out; a hooded bird will ride calmly on a perch in the back of the car.

Eventually the bird is taught to fly to the lure. The lure, a small leather pouch, is attached to a rope and swung over the falconer's head. The point is to entice the falcon to stoop to the lure, or fly down and hit the lure, in much the same way the bird will hit the prey. Many falconers attach a piece of meat or something like the wing of a duck to the lure, so the lure is always associated with food. The falconer lets the falcon catch or land on the lure. The idea is to train the bird to come in whenever it sees the lure swing. To a trained bird, the lure means food. The lure is mostly used with falcons. Shortwings and buteos— which are species of hawk—are considered birds of the fist, that is, birds that fly back to the fist for food.

At some point the falconer will have to let his bird fly free. This first flight is the one that gives a falconer pause: Is the bird ready to fly free? Will it come back to the lure? A falconer doesn't know the answers to those questions until he tries. Once falconer and falcon reach this milestone and then get beyond it, they can both concentrate on building the hunting partnership. If a falconer is flying a peregrine or a hybrid, his job is to train and encourage the bird to fly high into the sky above his head and then wait on, or circle above the falconer while he flushes game.

Most falconers keep some kind of hawking journal or log, recording at the very least the daily weight of the bird and the game taken. Birds are flown when they're a little on the light side, which indicates they might be hungry and more eager to hunt. Many hawking journals also record the events of the day's flight and often the weather conditions. They can be a pleasure to read because many convey a real sense of the passion a falconer feels toward his sport and his bird.

Today there are approximately forty-five hundred licensed falconers in the United States, and two to three thousand of them belong to NAFA. About four hundred falconers attend the annual NAFA meet, which is always held during the week of Thanksgiving somewhere in the midsection of the country where there's plenty of game for both those flying falcons (which prey on grouse, prairie chickens, pheasant, and duck) and those hawking with red-tailed hawks, Harris's hawks, and goshawks (which prey on cottontails, jackrabbits, and squirrels). One of the largest falconry clubs in the United States is the California Hawking Club; it was founded in the 1970s and has more than six hundred members. Their annual meet is one of the biggest in the country and can draw as many falconers as the NAFA meet, and sometimes more.

A very small percentage of the licensed falconers are long-wingers—those who fly falcons—like Steve and Tim. When I realized how few of them there were, I was shocked, and then I laughed at myself for being such an idiot. My falconry experience has been watching people fly peregrines and hybrid birds. But at a falconry meet, the majority of the falconers bring red-tails, Harris's hawks, or goshawks to fly. Although there are some falconers who train and fly different kinds of birds at the same time—falcons, buteos, and accipiters (sharp-shins, Cooper's hawks, and goshawks)—most don't. And falconers who fly particular kinds of birds tend to stick together—those who fly red-tails hang out with other hawkers who fly red-tails, and longwingers hang out with longwingers. It's my impression that the people flying falcons see themselves as the falconry elite (although they might not admit it) and are viewed by other hawkers as elitist. The bunny and squirrel hawkers—the majority of American falconers—don't have a whole lot of interest in watching the falcons fly, and the falconers certainly aren't interested in watching red-tails, Harris's hawks, and goshawks fly. Falconry is a teeny-tiny subculture within the American sporting and hunting scene, but even in such a small community, there can be divisions.

Ultimately, whether they're flying longwings or hawks, people become falconers because once they've been introduced to the sport, they can't imagine their lives without their birds. They form attachments to birds that can seem deeper than their attachments to other humans. They often raise these birds from chicks and then care for them—worry about them—until they die. I've heard many a falconer talk about losing a bird in such detail and with such passion that he gets himself into a state and has to end the conversation with "I can't talk about it anymore."

3
Wyoming

STEVE'S STORY IS a western story. His people have lived in the West for more than a hundred and fifty years. Steve rarely goes east, has no real desire to visit the East, and knows as surely as the sun sets in the west that there can be no good falconry in the East because there are no sage grouse there. One time Steve and I drove to Lehi, Utah, where Steve was giving a presentation at an Eagle Scout ceremony (his bald eagle, Liberty, was sitting on a perch in the back of the truck). In a tone of voice I didn't often hear him use—a tone that indicated he was really interested in the answer and not just being polite—he asked, "Is this what it looks like around where you live?" As we drove through the little town, with its broad streets and little bungalows that gave way to tract houses that stretched out into the desert, I looked around and said, "No." He really couldn't imagine a place like the little community that surrounds me in upstate New York, where Greek Revival and Victorian houses are set back from the road in tree-filled yards. Everything about it was different from where we were. "For one thing," I said as we passed a pasture with a couple of horses in it right in the middle of town, "that would never happen. We'd never have horses in a pasture in town. By the way, why does everyone in the West need to have a horse?" Now he looked at me with an expression of disbelief; he couldn't even answer the question because, in his western worldview, it was so stupid.

Steve's people were Mormon pioneers. His father's family were converts from Sweden who pushed their belongings across much of America during the great handcart migration in the 1850s. The Mormon leaders in newly formed Salt Lake City were so eager to get more people to the promised land they sent missionaries to Europe to convert people and bring them to America. There were more immigrants than the Mormon leadership had anticipated, so they decided to finance and organize ten companies of converts to push or pull all their belongings in handcarts a couple thousand miles from Illinois to Utah.

Between 1856 and 1860, almost 3,000 Mormons with 653 carts and 50 supply wagons traveled west. Each family was issued a two-wheeled cart with a box about three or four feet long and eight inches high. A cart could carry about five hundred pounds; each person was allotted seventeen pounds for personal possessions, and the rest of the weight was reserved for supplies. Most of the pioneers who came overland during the handcart migration made it, although two of the companies left Illinois late and were stranded in winter storms near Casper, Wyoming; hundreds died of exposure and starvation before rescue parties reached them.

One of Steve's maternal great-grandfathers, whose name was George Stringham, came west with Brigham Young as part of the Pioneer Band that set out from Nauvoo, Illinois, in 1846. Their job was to look for a permanent settlement site for the Latter-day Saints (another term for Mormons), who were being forced out of Illinois after the murder of their founder, Joseph Smith. Steve's great-grandfather George was with Brigham Young when Young stood at the mouth of the canyon that emptied into the Great Salt Lake Basin, pointed to the area that would become Salt Lake City, and proclaimed, "This is the place!" Later, George Stringham got extremely irritated with Brigham Young when George returned from a mission trip to England and found his family living with another family and all his possessions confiscated by the church.

"He was a very strong, powerful man—he was exceptionally strong—so when he came back and his family was living with another family and his children had rags for shoes because they had put everybody's possessions into the church, he was so upset he went up to Brigham Young and knocked him flat down. And Brigham Young would have sent Porter Rockwell, his equalizer, after him if it hadn't been for the people who loved my grandfather and knew him and told him to back off," said MJ, Steve's mother. "So he lost everything and moved to Brigham City and never did take off his garments [the undergarments Mormons wear signifying their religion] because he always said he had problems with the man and not the religion." Steve's great-grandfather George Stringham has been described as both extremely strong and a "ruffian." Before the falling-out, he'd often acted as a bodyguard for Brigham Young and the leaders of the early church.

These were Steve's people—these tough Mormon pioneers who were willing and able to make the arduous journey across America on foot. And I can certainly see that same pioneer spirit in Steve. Yeah, he likes comfort and the fact that he can jump into his Toyota truck and head out across Bureau of Land Management (BLM) land behind his house on a two-track road. But in the years before he'd bought the cabin outside of Eden, Wyoming, he had demonstrated the kind of pioneer stock he's descended from.

I used to think that Steve Chindgren would have made a perfect guide for a pioneer wagon train. I could see him riding ahead—a small, wiry man sitting perfectly erect on his horse, scouting out the territory and leading all those pioneers through the prairie and then the plains and then over the mountains to whatever promised land they decided upon. Or maybe he would have excelled as a nineteenth-century mountain man, scouring the mountains and valleys of the uncharted West for beaver and other game. Often these mountain men put themselves out of business because they so effectively and efficiently wiped out the game along their routes (that sounds like Steve), and they would then become guides because they had been all over hell's half acre and knew how to get there and back. Think about Kit Carson: he started out as a mountain man and then guided for John Frémont, who wrote a book about the Oregon Trail that made Kit Carson famous and opened up the West. Although, ultimately, Steve has a much better sense of what is right and what is wrong than Kit Carson did.

Like an early pioneer, Steve is driven by his need for land. Not just any land but wide-open landscape with lots of sagebrush on it. He doesn't have to own the land; he just has to have access to it for his hunting. And it's got to have the same qualities the pioneers looked for in their land. He needs land with pristine sources of water because without that, there'd be no game for him to hunt. And like another famous early pioneer, Daniel Boone, Steve has to have land that's away from other people. A decade after he got there, Daniel Boone left Boonesborough, Kentucky, a settlement he'd carved out of the wilderness, because, as he told someone, it was "too crowded."

Although half a million people traveled through Wyoming on the overland trails during the nineteenth century—trails that took them west to Oregon and California and Utah—few of them stopped to make the territory they traveled through their home. They stopped to let their cattle drink from the cool Wyoming creeks and eat the grass that grew along their banks. They came west over the Continental Divide through a low notch at the end of the Wind River Range called South Pass and then camped near creeks that ran in gullies through the high desert of what is now southwestern Wyoming. They made repairs to wagons and gave the horses and cattle a rest before continuing on. And when they resumed their journey, the people walked— only the very young, very old, or the very sick traveled in the wagons with the supplies—across what is now Wyoming, on their way to the promise of a better life.

Why didn't cities grow if there was water and grass and even trade opportunities with the settlers who were coming through? For one thing, the high alkali content of the water was tough on the cattle and the people. Today there are only half a million people in the entire state of Wyoming, giving it the distinction of being the least populated state in the nation; in 2007, partly because of its lack of people, Wyoming was voted the third most livable state. Ninety-one percent of the land is considered rural, and there are 230 days of sunshine a year. Okay, it can get cold—darn cold—and it is the windiest state in the country, but that's a small price to pay for all that open land. Should we consider Wyoming one of the last frontiers? A place on the map to be filled in only after both coasts are full? A place to raise cattle and mine minerals and reap the power of the wind with wind farms and pump natural gas and oil from the deep, deep earth?

In the last decade, Wyoming has become a kind of mecca for falconers. Sheridan, Wyoming, has a handful of rather famous falconers, including Bob Berry and Dan Konkel, men who breed and fly sleek and fast birds. Other falconers travel to Wyoming during the autumn. They bring their birds and dogs with them and spend their days hunting for sharp-tailed grouse and sage grouse in the vast tracts of public land overseen by the BLM. Steve has been coming to Wyoming for a couple of decades—first to camp on the banks of the Little Sandy, and later to stay in the cabin near Eden, Wyoming, a mere stone's throw from his old campsite. However, unlike most falconers, who come to Wyoming for a week to hunt, Steve is in Wyoming almost full-time during the falconry season. He works during the spring and summer; he's arranged his work schedule to accommodate his falconry schedule. Why have birds if you're not going to provide them with a hunting opportunity every single day during the season? He figures that wouldn't be fair to Jomo and Jahanna and the younger birds.

To get to Eden, which is in the southwestern part of the state, about forty-five miles north of the old Lincoln Highway or modern-day Interstate 30, you get off the main road in Rock Springs and drive north on Route 191. Or you can reach Eden by driving south on Route 191 from Pinedale. Either way, if you happen to get distracted for a moment by, say, looking at your map or fiddling with the radio, you won't notice Eden. Oh, you might see the Eden Bar, a concrete building painted sky blue in the front and sea-foam green on the sides with its sign that says *aloon* set in a rare grove of cottonwood trees. Or maybe you'll see the tiny brown-shingled pioneer church with the white steeple, across the road from the bar. And if you miss the bar and the church there's the convenience store—known locally as the feed store—with its green-painted plaster brontosaurus wearing a saddle that advertises an oil company from the era when this kind of a dinosaur was still called a brontosaurus.

If you happen to go into the feed store, you'll see it's much more than a convenience store: you can buy anything in there, from PVC piping for all your plumbing needs, oats for your horses, fence posts, bags of packaged gorp covered with a quarter of an inch of dust, hairbrushes, milk, beer, soda, toilet paper, two-pound bags of elbow macaroni, and corn dogs and burritos from under the heat lamps in the glass case at the counter. You can also learn the brands used by every cattle rancher in the area by studying the burned impressions in the wooden frieze running above the cooler doors.

And if you go just a touch farther north you'll pass the Country Burgers Café, where they serve everything in and on Styrofoam or paper plates but they still give you real silverware. Then barely a mile later you'll hit the town of Farson, and you'll know you're in Farson because there's Mitch's Café with its display case under the cash register holding an odd assortment of things for sale, including individual baseball cards, NFL cards, a cowboy poem written on what looks like a place mat for $20, one DVD for $10, several copies of a book of cowboy humor, one genuine antique rotating candy dish that looks like a little Ferris wheel, with cream-colored plastic containers the size of large clamshells. The sign says that it was made in 1951 and they want $100 for it. The last time I stopped in, there were also five dusty candy bars for sale.

The rest of Farson spills down Route 28 at the four corners. You'll pass by the low-slung brick post office, which is next door to the three-story brick building that first was a hotel and then a store where you could buy a wrench, Carhartt overalls, a hunting license, a pamphlet on the history of the region, watercolors, and an ice cream cone. But now, that business is gone and it's just the big brick building on the corner. On another corner is a gas station with the only ATM between Rock Springs and Pinedale. And if you stop to get gas and look across the way, you can just make out a historical marker saying that this was a stop on the Pony Express; it's next to another marker that points out the spot on the Little Sandy River where Brigham Young met Jim Bridger in 1847.

Farther down the road you'll pass the Oregon Trail Residential Park—a new trailer park for some of the hundreds of workers pouring into this part of the state to work in Jonah Field, the natural gas fields that begin at about highway marker 67 heading north on Route 191 toward Pinedale.

You'll find an interesting contrast in this part of Wyoming because gas wells are popping up like toadstools on a damp forest floor, and some of them are in close proximity to very visible reminders—such as deep ruts crossing the desolate desert—of the Oregon and Mormon trails. The pioneer history seems important to people, and they're fighting hard not to have gas wells and the Oregon Trail in the same view. This little part of the Oregon Trail on BLM land looks just how it did when the pioneers came through, and that makes it special.

ScheeeEE-oooo . . . scheeeEE-oooo . . . Bulky trucks with *EnCana* painted on their door panels rush by one after the other, carrying derrick pieces. It seems that all the drivers and passengers are wearing hardhats, even though they're riding in the trucks. The road seems way too busy for such a little ribbon of pavement slicing through the southwest corner of this big rectangular state. A local guy told me the road between Farson and Pinedale is one of the most dangerous stretches of highway in America—lots of fatal crashes from people trying to pass big trucks. Locally this stretch of road is known as the Jonah 500. On any given day, the road's shared by a surprising number of motorcyclists, recreational vehicles the size of Greyhound buses, a zillion pickup trucks, trucks pulling horse trailers, trucks with bulk tanks warning you to stay back, oversize loads of half-houses careening down the highway, and flatbeds with heavy equipment strapped and chained and bolted to the beds. Occasionally a group of startled pronghorn begins to run parallel to the road and then veers sharply toward the sagebrush desert, their white rumps undulating like a string of Christmas lights blowing in a stiff breeze. Off in the distance, little specks of white and brown and black cattle pick around the sagebrush, searching for something to eat.

So here we are—in the West. Where grazing rights on public land are fiercely protected. Where cattle and pronghorn and elk and mule deer and sage grouse all compete for limited water and food on the land we all own. Where you can own the land your house is built on but you may not have the rights to what lies in the ground beneath it. Where natural gas wells are sprouting like dandelions after a storm and are all connected by an intricate web of dirt roads—and sometimes paved ones—threading through the high green and brown desert that stretches as far as the eye can see in every direction.

Historian Richard White wrote, "When Americans tell stories about themselves, they set those stories in the West. American heroes are Western heroes, and when you begin to think of the quintessential American characters, they're always someplace over the horizon. There's always someplace in the West where something wonderful is about to happen. . . . And even when we turn that around . . . even when we say, 'Well, something has been lost,' what's lost is always in the West."

Steve has a photograph in the cabin—it's just a small picture in a cheap wooden frame—in which he's standing in the doorway of the Scamp. It's winter, and the scene is predominantly white except for the scrubby-looking gray-green bushes heading up the bank behind the Scamp. Even the sky is a shade of blue-white. The Scamp is white, with the word *Scamp* written in stylized red letters on the side beneath the window. Two falcons, Tava and Jomo, are perched out on block perches, and a black-and-white dog, probably Annie, is sniffing the ground. Written on the front of the photo in gold is *Last camp, Dec. 2001.*

Steve has been coming to Wyoming to hunt sage grouse for about twenty years but has owned the cabin only since 2002. Before that he chose to bring his housing with him rather than stay in the little motel in Farson, a one-story six-room building right next to Mitch's Café. A woman named Mickey owned both establishments for years—the café's been in the family since 1951. Recently she sold the café to her son-in-law and daughter, who, according to a local guy, are running it into the ground.

"They can't get no help," he said, probably because they can't compete with the oil and gas companies up the road. The café has erratic hours these days, often closed even when it's supposed to be open, and it's now officially closed all day Sunday and Monday.

The first winter Steve came to Wyoming—Jomo's first hunting season—he'd pulled the used thirteen-foot Scamp trailer behind his truck. He'd bought the Scamp so he could camp in Park Valley, about a hundred and fifty miles northwest of his home near Salt Lake, and do several days of hawking at a time. When he lost his hunting license in Utah, Steve loaded up the Scamp and headed to Wyoming and the Farson area, which is about a four-hour drive from Salt Lake. He set his trailer down on the banks of the Little Sandy, a stone's throw from the Oregon Trail—the route his great-grandfather had taken a hundred and sixty years earlier as he made his way to the Great Salt Lake and the promised land—and established his own grouse camp.

Steve's pasted some photos of the Scamp days into his falconry journal. I love the ones showing the Scamp plunked down in either the dry grass or the snow with lawn chairs set up outside the door, inviting tired falconers to take in a bit of the afternoon sun. There's a picture of Steve with no shirt on sitting in some kind of collapsible container and pouring a bucket of snow over his head. It's labeled *Snow Bath Dec. 01*. There's also a very sweet photo of a grouse dinner held in the Scamp with four people crammed around the table and Steve in the foreground kneeling and grinning for the camera. If there were any more than four people, dinner had to be eaten in shifts.

During autumn the Scamp must have been a fun place to stay. Sure, quarters were cramped and the area where the table was doubled as the space for the bed, but it was nice for Steve to have a home away from home. And after a morning of hawking it was so pleasant to come back to the camp on a wide spot on the creek and stake out the birds and the dogs and get out the lawn chair and soak in the warm midday sun. Winter, however, was another story.

"It took a lot to be able to stick it out in the winter," said Steve. "I was never quite sure if I was hard-core or stupid by doing that."

He had a routine that helped him make it through the winter hunting months. Because the heater in the trailer didn't work, when Steve went hawking in the afternoon he would open up all the windows and put a propane heater in the center of the trailer. When he'd come back from the field, he'd know where the trailer was before he even reached the Little Sandy because he'd see a plume of steam rising from the creek bed. And as he came along the two-track, he'd see his trailer, sometimes covered with snow except for the bare part of the roof where the snow had melted because of the heater. Then he'd go inside and shut off the heater and close the windows, and the Scamp would stay warm enough for the rest of the day. There were two propane cook burners in the Scamp, and most nights he'd fix a quick meal and then place a kettle of water on one of the burners, ready to be heated in the morning. About once a week he'd splurge and go for an evening meal at the café.

After dinner he'd strip down to his long underwear and crawl into his big sleeping bag and then cover himself with wool blankets, leaving a hole just big enough for him to breathe through. In the morning the sleeping bag would be caked with so much ice around the breathing hole that it was sometimes hard to break open. The morning routine was to jump out of bed, light the propane heater and open the windows wide (so he wouldn't die from the fumes), light the burner under the kettle of frozen water, then get back into the sleeping bag until the kettle was ready. He had to sleep with the disposable lighter inside his sleeping bag or else it would get so cold the lighter wouldn't work. When the kettle was hot, he'd get out of bed again, wet some paper towels with the hot water, and take a sponge bath.

Then he'd get dressed. By this point in the morning Steve was fully awake and ready to go. He'd load the dogs and birds into the back of the truck, make sure he had his telemetry equipment, then head off for a hot cup of coffee and a place to warm his hands at the café in Farson. He got to know the 6:00 A.M. crowd pretty well—as in many little diners all over rural America, the same group of men sat at the same tables every morning.

When guests came to go hawking with Steve in the winter, they'd stay at the motel in Farson. One year, a friend, Al Gardner, decided to stay at the Scamp on a night Steve wasn't going to be there.

"Al told me it got to thirty below zero that night and he had to get into his car and start it up to get warm," said Steve. "He said he didn't know how I did it and was tempted to write *Al Gardner almost died here* on the wall of the Scamp. To me it was home—I had it fixed up pretty good." He paused, then said, "I thought it was kind of neat that I could live in a thing like that in one of the harshest, coldest places in the country."

He spent fourteen winter seasons in Wyoming, living in the Scamp five days a week, every week, for months, and going home to Utah on the weekends.

4

Eden

AT SOME POINT, Steve hit the wall. He thought, *What the hell am I doing living in the Scamp?* and knew he had to make a plan. He had fallen in love with Wyoming, particularly the Eden area, with its view of the Wind River Range off to the north—a range of sharp edges and broad mountain faces—and the expansive, open vista showing a gray-green carpet of sage in every other direction. Between the mountains and the cabin is the Big Sandy River. The Little Sandy flows into the Big Sandy, which meanders through the sage, confined by widely spaced banks—bluffs, really—that hint at the river's hidden intermittent power. Many afternoons the wind comes whipping through the region, picking up dust and dirt and gravel and snow and spreading it about, but Steve doesn't care. He loves the area, and he loves the fact that there could conceivably be a sage grouse behind every bush.

Then he found it. Next to a huge swath of BLM land west of Eden, not half a mile from where he parked his Scamp, a cabin came on the market. He knew he couldn't afford to buy the place on his own, so he made a video of the property and sent it to a couple of wealthy falconers he had gotten to know over the years. One of them, David Kennedy, from Georgia, took Steve up on the offer.

They bought the house and twenty acres for $160,000. "It's

worth a lot more now," said Steve. Always thinking about the next move that would let him spend more time in Wyoming, Steve said, "It'd be the perfect place to bring people to see spring grouse. It could be like a bed-and-breakfast. I took some hardcore birders out there last year to see some birds strutting, and it was pretty nice. They watched the grouse for about an hour."

Steve's wife, Julie, wasn't too pleased that Steve took their life savings and put it into the place, but Steve's attitude is that it's just money, and he knows they'll get their investment back and then some. If the place burned down tomorrow, Steve thinks, it would have been worth it because of the amount of pleasure he's gotten from it.

Over the past several years, the cabin has turned into the kind of falconry lodge Steve always imagined owning. He calls it the House of Grouse. When they bought the place, it was a wreck. Orange shag carpet covered the floors, and at one point a door had blown open and a coyote had killed a jackrabbit in front of the fireplace in the living room and then stashed part of the remains in the bathtub. But it was a solid structure sitting on twenty acres of land abutting thousands of acres of BLM land, which offered the promise of no neighbors and potentially lots of game. David fronted most of the money for the improvements and furnishings for the lodge, and Steve acts as caretaker.

David and his friends and family use the lodge several times a year for hunting parties and family get-togethers. David is a falconer, but he's also a gun hunter, as are his sons. A couple of years ago David purchased several horses and had a pole barn constructed out back behind the cabin; he hired the closest neighbor to feed and exercise the animals when he's not in town. The whole arrangement suits Steve quite well because that means for about eleven months out of the year he has the cabin to himself and whomever he wants to entertain.

In fact, at this point, so many people know about the falconry lodge and want to come visit, Steve's in a bit of a bind. On the one hand, he loves to show off the cabin, but on the other hand, people tend to come and treat it like a vacation house, with Steve acting as guide, cook, and housekeeper. Steve can't seem to find a balance.

Like everyone else, I love the cabin. It's a low-slung log structure with an attached two-car garage on one end and a porch stretching across the front. The main block is large and open and holds a kitchen, dining area, and massive living room. The two wings, one on either side of the main block, have a total of three bedrooms, two baths, and a laundry room. There's also a finished basement that accommodates four or five more hunters, dormitory style, and a bathroom with a shower. There's a hot tub outside on a deck through the sliding doors in Steve's bedroom. It's everything Steve has ever wanted.

David cut the check and told Steve to furnish the place. Steve bought leather couches and chairs; a Mission oak dining set that seats ten; the latest in kitchen appliances; and pine-log beds outfitted with extra-thick mattresses and down comforters. It has a Ralph Lauren meets Eddie Bauer meets Crate and Barrel look.

In the glass-fronted bookcase along one wall of the dining area are about a hundred black, red, and brown leather falcon hoods of varying sizes; you could fit the head of anything from a merlin to an eagle. They all have elaborate topknots made from leather, feathers, or wool. Some of the hoods sit on white ceramic hood molds. Placed among the hoods are hawking artifacts and funky advertisements, including an empty Falcon Beer can from Germany; Hawk Aftershave by Mennen; an unopened pack of Falcon Lights menthol cigarettes; a dozen brass hawking bells; an Arabian falconry cuff; and books by falconers and about falconry, including a translation of Frederick II's *The Art of Falconry*.

Prints and paintings and drawings and lithographs of falcons and sage grouse hang on every single knotty-pine-and-log wall in the cabin. A chandelier made of a dozen entwined deer antlers sits above the oak dining room table, throwing a soft light over the warm, open-grained wood. Four taxidermied grouse hang from the living room ceiling by monofilament, arranged in a somewhat frightening tableau of permanent flight, and there's a matte black pellet stove jammed into the massive orange lichen–covered-rock fireplace whose chimney shoots up through the middle of the cabin. On the wide wood-plank mantel are memorial photographs of birds killed by eagles and owls. A wooden House of Grouse mirror made by the Famous Grouse whiskey distillery hangs near the front door. The overstuffed leather couches and chairs are so deep you can't lean back while keeping your feet on the floor unless you're over six feet tall, and there's a bronze of a slightly larger-than-life falcon on the fist near the wide-screen television. A resin statue of a buffalo sits on a low coffee table that sits on a buffalo skin in front of one of the leather couches. And wood is everywhere, whether it's barely skinned half logs, knotty-pine siding, or rough-hewn exposed rafters. It's a constant reminder that this is a manly hunting cabin stuck in the manly hunting West.

The front porch's uneven floorboards hold several willow chairs with cushions bungee-corded to them so they won't blow away in the winds that come whipping off the open land in front of the house. A hummingbird feeder filled with sugar water hangs from a rafter on the front porch and attracts the rufous hummingbirds that cruise through from their nesting areas in the Wind River Range. They probably come off the mountains and make a beeline across BLM land right to the house because they perceive the bright red metal roof as an enormous patch of flowers. They fly, dart, and hover at this oasis of sugar water they find in the dry desert.

The attached garage isn't for vehicles; it serves as a falconry and fly-fishing staging area with built-in wall perches for four birds, and racks to hold fly rods. Several nicely tooled leather saddles sit on sawhorses, with the leather and nylon tack neatly hung on pegs along one wall. A couple of overturned canoes sit in the garage rafters.

Along the hallway to the garage is a gallery of framed photographs of the falconers and their birds who have spent time in the Wyoming falconry lodge as guests of Steve and David. It's like a who's who of falconry or a falconry hall of fame as the faces of Heinz Meng, Colonel Kent Carnie, and Tom Cade silently stare from their frozen poses. A special place on the wall is reserved for those intrepid falconers and their birds who brave the winter and make kills in the cold, snowy conditions of the high desert around Eden. Men with birds on their fists stand in the open western landscape, dead grouse at their feet. All are captured in a timeless freeze-frame by Steve's camera.

I love sitting on the front porch of the cabin with a cup of coffee in my hand looking out across the dirt road toward the wide-open spaces and the Wind River Range about fifty miles away. Mile after mile of slightly undulating semi-arid land with knee-high sagebrush stretches as far as I can see. If I squint my eyes, the muted greens and browns soften and blur the prickly edges of the sagebrush, making the desert seem safe and soft and welcoming. I feel as if I could wade through the bushes and somehow reach those distant mountains.

But if you peel back that faux softness and take a closer look, you'll see a harsher landscape, one that hides old bottles and tin cans and pieces of wire—things tossed from trucks, from horseback, from wagons. And you'll see ruts made by wagons and even handcarts as tens of thousands of Mormons and other pioneers made their way west in the mid-nineteenth century. You'll see graves marked with rocks and slabs of wood, and you can find big chunks of petrified wood and arrowheads and spear points, some dating back almost ten thousand years. But you have to look closely to see these things.

When Steve peels back the layers, he sees thousands and

thousands of sage grouse hiding in the sagebrush—big brown-and-white birds that feed off the musky green leaves. Chicken-sized birds that can make themselves practically invisible by not moving and almost hugging the ground as a predator draws near. They instinctively know that safety is in the cover of the sage. And although sage grouse are powerful flyers and have tremendous stamina once they get going, they face the risk of getting slammed by a raptor, most likely a golden eagle, the minute they leave the safety of the sage.

A lot of the locals don't really know what to make of Steve. They see him at the café and the feed store and the post office. They look at his framed photos of sage grouse and pronghorn and local landmarks like Jack Morrow Hills that line the walls of Mitch's Café. They see him driving every single two-track road that cuts through the prickly desert. They chitchat with him, but as so often happens in small towns in rural America, they don't really know Steve. He'll always be the guy who owns the place a couple miles west of Eden.

"A lot of the locals think I'm kind of an environmentalist. They want to kill all the wolves, poison everything that might bother the livestock, shoot all the eagles—that's just the way the ranchers think. Most of them, anyway. Anything they think threatens their livelihood they want to get rid of, and that's something that's been passed on for generations and generations," said Steve. "Their forefathers worked awfully hard to get rid of wolves. Most of the reputation of the wolf probably comes from coffee shops, but I know there are people who do lose animals to them. But they lose animals to bad weather too.

"I saw a dead raven over by the Big Sandy yesterday and I wondered if it was West Nile virus or if it had been shot. Everyone up here hates ravens. If you mention ravens in the coffee shop they'll say, 'Oh, those bloodthirsty things, they pick the eyes out of the calves,' and they all say that. I think someone said that once and it just spread throughout the West. I've seen ravens around cows when they're giving birth and the cow won't let them get anywhere near the calf," said Steve. "But it gives the ranchers a chance to hate ravens."

Steve works hard to stay friendly with the locals; he's very affable but keeps a low profile. Most of them know he's a falconer because he's been coming to the area for twenty years. They call him "That bird guy who has the house out there." If people from Farson come to the zoo in Salt Lake, he gives them free passes, and they think that's pretty neat.

5

Steve and Julie

STEVE AND JULIE'S HOUSE is tucked into the elbow of a dead-end street in Centerville, Utah. This is only the second house Steve has ever lived in—he moved from the canyon where he'd grown up to this house in what was then a small town about ten miles north of Salt Lake City. Now it's connected to the city by a ten-lane freeway that's jammed with cars during both ends of the workday.

The house is low slung and sand colored in a development of low-slung, sand-colored houses. In mid-July, in the midst of a heat wave, the front yard is lush and green and completely edged with a bed chock-full of short-stemmed red, orange, and pink zinnias. Big sand-colored planters drip yellow and purple pansies. To the right of the attached garage is the chainlink dog pen where the dogs lie on their sides in unmoving lumps, trying to beat the heat. A high privacy fence surrounds the small back-yard. From the deck off the kitchen, which is on the upper floor of the split-level house, you can sit amid the big pots of impatiens on a comfy deck chair and look down on the enclosed yard. It's not like any other backyard in the neighborhood. It contains an intricate collection of small attached buildings—mews—and outdoor pens, which hold all manner of raptors and zoo birds during the off-season. In midsummer the mews hold Steve's personal falconry birds, including Jomo, who is busy feeding and rearing four gyr-peregrine hybrids. The chicks and the mother were in the pen next to Jomo's, and as soon as he saw those chicks he began to try to feed them. Eventually Steve left the door open between the pens and now they're all playing one big happy family. Later in the summer Steve will choose two of the birds he wants to keep and will give away or sell the other two. In the meantime, Jomo's as into parenting at age twenty as he was when he was just a young thing.

Walnuts, a teenager of a brown-and-white rooster, had the run of the place. First he was in the backyard, then he was on the deck going beak to nose with the big black-and-white housecat, the sliding glass door to the kitchen between them. Walnuts was one of two thousand cockerel chicks that had come home from the hatchery that spring; he'd been spared the fate of becoming hawk food, but the rest of the chicks were shoved into a plastic bag with a bit of dry ice, which sucked out all the oxygen.

As we ate dinner and drank beers on the deck, the triple-digit temperature went down by a few degrees. In the large bare lot directly behind the house, a backhoe and a large earthmover lumbered back and forth, making the constant *eeeeRRRR* and grinding noises that only huge machinery can. Two months ago there had been a plant nursery there, and the Chindgrens had believed, erroneously as it turned out, that they would be protected from backyard neighbors forever. At dinner, as we talked over the *eeeeRRRR eeeeRRRR eeeeRRRR*, they contemplated what was going to happen when a yard abutted their fence. Steve wondered if the zoning people were going to come after him. He expected they would, which would cause a crisis because Steve and Julie make their living from the birds that are in their backyard and in their garage at least six months out of the year. When all the birds are there from the zoo, it's a real menagerie, complete with jungle noises. Those are not the kind of neighborhood sounds that new homeowners want to hear.

Julie is a beautiful woman in her late forties with shoulder-length brown hair and a killer body that she keeps in perfect shape by doing aerobics in the basement and by staying away from sugar and complex carbohydrates. Their two daughters, Jenna and Jessie, are also beautiful. In fact, when the whole family is together, they look downright wholesome in that all-American way, with perfectly straight gleaming white teeth and gorgeous heads of hair ranging from very blond (Jenna) to reddish blond (Steve) to light brown (Julie) to chestnut brown (Jessie). And as often happens in families with two kids, each kid resembles one of the parents. Jenna, who's twenty-one, is the spitting image of photos I've seen of Steve when he was in his twenties, and Jessie, who's eighteen, looks just like Julie.

In the fall, Jessie will be attending a state school a couple of hours south of Salt Lake City; she thinks she might major in English or business. For the summer she's working at a credit union, where she shreds documents and does whatever else needs doing. She seems like a typical teenager with a car and cell phone and all the other stuff kids have today.

Jenna attends the University of Utah and during the summer works for Steve at the zoo, where she helps weigh and feed the birds and has a comic part in the bird show. She pretends to be a volunteer from the audience who ends up in a shallow pool when some doves fly past her. It's pretty funny, and the girl does a very graceful backward pratfall, which doesn't surprise me because she clearly has genetically endowed athleticism.

Julie and Steve have been married for more than twenty years, and I asked Julie what it was like to be married to and have a family with someone who was essentially gone six months out of the year.

"At first it was really hard," she said. "But I knew falconry was his passion when I married him and that I wasn't going to change that. He was never going to be home in the fall and winter. It was really hard when the girls were little, but when they got older and into school and they got so busy, we just fell into a routine. They'd come home from school and we'd sit at the kitchen table and do homework, and later, when they were in sports and all those activities, I spent most of my time driving them around.

"In fact, when Steve came home at times when we didn't expect him, it made it more difficult," she added. "Those are the times we'd have trouble."

Steve hadn't wanted to have kids, but Julie did, so they'd compromised. "She could have her two daughters, which is what she always wanted, and it would be her job to stay at home and take care of them because I wasn't going to do it," said Steve. He absolutely adores his daughters and seems quite amazed that he could produce such beautiful beings. ("None of their friends have a father who will text message them 'I love you,'" he told me.)

Julie said that she'd known what the deal was from the beginning, and when it got tough, her only option was to get out if she didn't like it. She'd gotten used to Steve being gone. "A little too used to it," she said. She's very close to her sister, who lives five minutes away, and has a big group of friends she does things with. Julie has taught aerobics classes at night in the basement of the house since the girls were little and joked that the aerobics ladies were her husband because they heard about everything the kids did during the day and they gave her advice and acted like her support group.

"You get so used to living the way you live, with him being gone year after year," said Julie. "And every year it's the same thing. We get used to him being gone in the fall and the winter, so when he actually starts being home in the spring, it's a hard adjustment for him and for us. Every year this happens. You'd think we'd catch on. And as the kids got older they had homework and games and I was so busy with them that when he was gone it was a relief because it was one more thing I didn't have to think about."

Julie recognized how hard it was for him to get back into the routine of family life. "We made it work," she said. "You couldn't have stopped him from going away. It was either make it work or . . . you know. When he first started going away I decided this was going to be my time as well and that I was going to have fun because he was up there having fun. I didn't want to feel resentful. So I had some fun, even if it was just taking a tub at night. And now I can't imagine doing it any other way.

"Now when he comes home on weekends I know it'll be this big fun thing where we'll go out and see friends and then he'll leave again and I'll go back to my daily schedule. And then it'll be the weekend again and it'll be fun all over again."

Now that the kids are older, Steve's ready for them to leave home and for Julie to join him at least part of the time in the cabin during the autumn. But she won't do it.

"She won't come to the cabin unless there are several couples going and it's going to be a party," said Steve. Julie said she's bored there without other people around and that there's nothing to do.

There's no doubt about it being seriously isolated—you can look in three directions and see nothing but sagebrush desert stretching to the horizon, like a big prickly blanket. Then in the fourth direction, down the washboard road that ends at Steve's cabin, you can see a barn and a bit of a trailer peeking out from behind some big old cottonwood trees. Those are the neighbors. If you have a hankering to go out, you can stop at the Eden Bar at the other end of the road and drink beer with the roustabouts who are working on the rigs and maybe, if you're feeling adventurous, shoot some pool. Julie delights in more urban pleasures, such as going to good restaurants and having a grocery store within a reasonable driving distance. She's not into getting her meat at the all-purpose convenience store/gas station/animal-feed store on the way to Farson.

Steve periodically mentions the fact that Julie won't go with him when he flies his birds, not even when they're up at the cabin and other wives are going out. He thinks she'd have fun just standing by the truck and looking at the desert, but clearly she thinks otherwise.

"She's never gone out hawking with me. Well, she may have gone out with me when the kids were little, but she probably stayed in the car," Steve said. "I don't think she's ever come out with me and watched me fly my birds because she doesn't want to see a kill. I told her you have to walk over there to see the bird on a kill. You don't really see it."

When I visited with Steve's mother, MJ, she told me about the night Steve had spent on a mountain after one of the young birds he'd been training for his bird show flew off toward a distant ridge. Steve headed out with his telemetry equipment and walked up and up and up, tracking the bird's signal. He didn't have anything with him—no cell phone, water, or warm clothes—but was single-mindedly focused on getting his bird back. When he got to the top of the ridge, it was night and dark as could be. He knew by the strength of the telemetry signal that his bird was only about forty yards away, but he couldn't risk trying to get it in the dark because he didn't want to spook it. So he sat down to wait for dawn.

In the meantime, Julie was frantic and called the search and rescue squad. "I told her, 'I know you're worried and I'm worried too but I don't think you should call search and rescue.' But she was so upset," said MJ. "I knew that he knew every inch of the mountain and would be okay."

Steve saw bobbing flashlights coming up the mountain and guessed what had happened. When they got within shouting range, he yelled, "Go home! I'm not leaving until I get my bird!"

In the early-morning light he made his way to the beeping transmitter, but all he found was a pile of feathers and one of the transmitters. The bird had been nailed by an eagle. Steve went back down the mountain, passing the base camp several hundred yards below the ridge where the search and rescue team had been set up. Julie didn't say a word to him for a week after that, she was so angry.

"I have a feeling that up to that point she loved me a lot more than she does now. I think that was a turning point," Steve said quietly. "I think she tries not to be quite so attached because of the way I am.

"I would like to live in the cabin. I have this vision that when the kids are gone Julie will come with me during the hawking season and stay with me while I'm hawking. But it's never going to happen," he said. "It's sad because I just want to be with her more. I know that when the kids are gone, she's still not going to come up there. She's gonna say, 'I'm not going up there because I don't like it up there.' And there's nothing I can do about it."

6

Winter Hawking

DURING THE MONTHS of December and January, sage grouse can be the most difficult quarry to hunt with a falcon. At that point in the year, the grouse are seasoned—they're strong flyers, they're in big flocks on their wintering grounds, and they spook so easily that hunting them with falcons is much more difficult than it usually is. But because Steve's been observing the birds for almost two decades, he knows the location of all the sage grouse wintering grounds in his part of Wyoming, places where hundreds of hen and cock birds spend their days feeding on sagebrush leaves.

This morning, like every morning in the cabin, Steve gets up early—though in the winter he sleeps in until 5:30 A.M.—and after stretching to try to get his body working properly, he walks stiffly from his bedroom to the kitchen, snapping on a few lights along the way. He begins to make the coffee, using water from the big water cooler in the pantry because the water from the well is so full of minerals it's not really fit to drink. Then he checks the temperature gauge in the window over the kitchen sink. Ten degrees above zero. Fifteen percent humidity. It didn't snow overnight—too dry to snow—so it might not be too difficult to drive to most of the wintering grounds to check for grouse. Yesterday, the snow depth ranged from nothing to two feet, depending on where he was relative to where the wind blew. In areas protected from the punishing Wyoming wind, the snow tends to pile up, while in great open areas whole sections of the desert are blown clean. You can often tell which way the prevailing wind is blowing by looking at the snow gathered on the lee side of the sagebrush.

While the coffee brews, Steve pulls out the toaster, puts in a couple of slices of cinnamon raisin bread—his favorite breakfast—and pushes the lever down. He lets it toast while he heads down the hall, past the wall of fame. He stops to put his down vest on over the long johns, blue jeans, and flannel shirt he's already wearing, then steps into his lined work boots. Entering the garage-turned-mews, he turns on the light, and the four birds tethered to wall perches perk up.

He starts to talk to his birds in a low voice as he moves across the cement floor. The words don't seem important; rather it's the low, silky timbre that seems to make them sit a little higher on their perches, perhaps in anticipation of the hunt that will surely follow. He pulls a well-worn falconry glove made from kangaroo leather onto his left hand and approaches the first bird. After untying one end of the leash, he places his gloved hand out for the bird to step up onto. He carries him over to the balance scale and puts the bird down on the perch. He unthreads the leash from the bracelets that hold it to the bird's legs. He doesn't want any extra weight on the bird. Then he carefully weighs him and records the weight in grams in a notebook he keeps next to the scale. He takes the bird back to his wall perch; places its hood over its head; carefully tightens the braces with his teeth and the fingers of his right hand, the way falconers have done for centuries; and then repeats this process with each of the other three birds.

He returns to the cabin and walks past the wall of fame, past the brewed coffee, past the now-cold toast, and down the rear hallway to the room where the dogs stay during the cold weather. Tucker and Earl (David's hunting dog) are standing up and whining just a little as Steve opens the door and then crosses the room to let them out the back. They bolt and start exploring the yard—running and wiggling and sniffing—while Steve finishes his chores.

He enters the kitchen and peers out the window, not seeing even a hint of daylight yet. *Good,* he thinks. He pushes the toast back down into the toaster for a warm-up and pours himself a cup of coffee. The toast pops up and he butters it and eats it while leaning against the gray faux-granite counter. When he's finished, he wipes the counter clean, pushes the toaster back against the wall, and turns off the coffeepot.

Steve grabs his keys and goes out the back door to the truck that's parked three feet away. He starts it to get it warmed up. On the way through the garage, he picks up a headlamp, puts it on, and turns on the powerful little beam of light that comes from the two AAA batteries. It's really cold and dark out, and when he looks up he sees thousands of stars, like white pinpricks in the inky black Wyoming sky. He opens the back of the truck, pushes aside the two long perches for the birds, and whistles for the dogs. They come bounding over, tails wagging and noses sniffing, and Tucker puts his front paws up on the tailgate. "Come on, Tuckie boy . . . you're a good boy . . . kennel up," says Steve. Tucker jumps into the truck and goes into his wooden box and sits down on the bedding. Steve shuts the kennel door. He claps his hands together to get them warmed up a little—he hates wearing gloves and can't really wear them anyway when he has a falconry glove on. Earl is much more reluctant to hop into the truck and has to be lifted up and placed into the truck bed. Once up there, he goes into his kennel and lies down on the bedding. Steve shuts his kennel door.

Now he has to get the birds loaded. One by one he takes the birds from the garage, brings them to the truck, and sets them on the AstroTurf-covered perch in the truck bed. Jomo gets loaded last because he will be the first bird to fly.

Steve makes one more swing through the house. He gets any crumbs he missed in his first cleanup, makes sure the coffee-pot is off, turns out the lights, and heads back to the truck. By this time the truck is getting toasty. The radio's tuned to the station from Rock Springs and is playing country songs about men leaving women, women leaving men, and soldiers fighting for the honor of the USA in Iraq—*Eye-rack*. Between every couple of songs there's a weather report; Steve turns the volume up to hear it, then turns it back down when the report's over. He looks in on the dogs and birds in the back, and before shutting the tailgate and closing the back window he checks to be sure he has some dead sparrows—sparrows he caught in a wire-mesh trap he set by the pigeon coop the day before—in his canvas hawking bag to feed the falcons after their flights. He also throws in a big bottle of water for the dogs. Then he stands with his driver's door open—*ding ding ding ding*—and rummages around behind his seat, making sure he has his telemetry equipment for the birds and his shock collars and telemetry for the dogs. He checks the batteries of each collar. There's nothing worse than sending a dog out and then realizing you can't track him because the collar has dead batteries.

Finally, it's time to leave. It's about 6:10, which gives him almost an hour before the sun comes up. This will give him plenty of time to gas up the Toyota at the feed store and then find grouse somewhere on the thousands of snow-covered BLM acres surrounding Eden and Farson.

Snow crystals swirl, sometimes forming tight funnels that spring up from the desert floor and other times spreading themselves thin over wide swaths of land, like a gossamer blanket of reflected and refracted early-morning light. This particular morning the wind, ever present, comes down off the mountains and sweeps across the high desert plains of a place Steve calls Rocky Flats, in honor of his falcon Rocky, who was killed there by a golden eagle several years ago. Sometimes this early in the day there isn't any wind at all, which in southwestern Wyoming in January is a blessing, but this morning there is enough of a breeze to pick up the top layer of light dry, powdery snow that covers the desert floor and send it flying. In places, the snow is piled up in two- and even three-foot drifts; in others, it's hard to tell where the snow ends and the hard-packed desert of abraded quartz crystals and pebbles made from volcanic rocks and minerals begins, because both the ephemeral and the longer-lasting crystals pick up and hold the early-morning rays of light.

Steve drove along the two-track road that crossed the BLM land heading into Rocky Flats. Four-wheel drive is necessary in this part of Wyoming if you intend to go off the paved roads. Steve was really glad he had it because at times he dipped down into ditches and creek gullies. Getting into a ditch was easy, but he had to floor it and aim the truck at just the right angle to climb the opposite bank. Sometimes his truck acted like a plow, and he sent snow flying when he hit the snowdrifts dead on, where they covered the road.

I imagined the ride the four hooded falcons were having, sitting on the perches in the back of the truck. From years of experience, the birds knew to grip the AstroTurf tightly as Steve bumped along the two-track heading into Rocky Flats. It was already 6:55, and the sun had just inched above the Wind River Range.

Steve drove slowly, looking for sage grouse tracks in the snow. He knew just what to look for—little paths of three-toed tracks that went round and round the low sagebrush bushes. He'd seen the crazy circular pattern of their tracks from a small plane he'd hired a couple of years earlier to search for the wintering grounds of the sage grouse. As he drove, he also scanned for large dark-colored birds sitting on the tops of the sagebrush. Like bathers on a beach, the birds liked to catch a few rays as the sun hit the desert.

"Sage grouse really fly well at this time of year," he said as we bounced along. "But hunting them successfully also depends on terrain. When we hunt sage grouse in Idaho the sage is higher there, and when falcons try to hunt them the grouse put into the brush rather than fly. That's a mistake on their part because falcons can go in and get them pretty easy then because, unlike pheasants, sage grouse are really bad in cover.

"The thing that makes hunting a sage grouse hard up here is that they can outfly your birds. The way I look at it, whenever someone argues with me and says the sage grouse aren't tough to catch up here because they've caught sage grouse with their birds, I say, 'Well, did your bird catch the grouse in a tail chase or clean in a stoop?'" (Meaning, Did the bird have to chase the grouse across the desert and over hill and dale before killing it or did he kill it by plummeting from the sky and striking the grouse so hard it bounced off the desert floor?)

He downshifted as we left the well-defined two-track and headed across what looked to me like open desert. As we bounced along, snow flying behind the truck, he added, "If you have to use your telemetry to find your bird down on a grouse, then you really shouldn't count that as a good flight."

We'd rode in silence for a few more minutes, then Steve said, "You dream of places like this throughout your whole falconry career. You fly around places with fences and telephone poles, things that can hurt your birds—and a lot of guys who live around civilization do that—then to be able to hunt in a place like this—well, it's amazing. It scares the guys who come here to fly and are used to flying in agricultural fields. They say, 'What if my bird takes off? There are no roads.' And I tell them you can get around down here. It's not like there are paved roads with signs on them, though."

What eventually becomes clear to me is that it really comes down to the kind of falconry experience you want to have. Steve realizes that the falconers who come to Wyoming and fly great big female hybrids or female gyrfalcons are going to have an easier time catching sage grouse than someone flying a tiercel, or male, hybrid. The males are about two-thirds the size of the females. This reverse sexual dimorphism occurs in many raptor species, and although no one really knows why, it's believed to have something to do with nesting. For example, the female stays with the young, and because she's larger, she can better defend the young against predators. Also, when the chicks are very young they require more nutritious food—such as sparrows—which are more easily caught by the smaller, more aerial males. Biologist and longtime falconer Jim Enderson writes about the behavior he's seen while visiting peregrine nests: "In a way, male and female peregrines are distinct kinds of birds. Males are much quicker and more aerial. They tend to be away hunting when people visit eyries. In defense males tend to go higher and dive faster at intruders, but they seldom attack. Females may land on the next ledge and walk right up to an intruding human, ready for battle."

These days Steve flies only tiercel hybrids, and with that comes a certain snobbery when he talks about flying his birds on sage grouse.

"If you're not worried about style," he said, "you can fly a big female hybrid or a gyrfalcon on sage grouse. I've made it as difficult for myself as possible because I want to do it right and catch them clean if I can." He paused and then added, "It's a hard thing to do."

The challenge for Steve is to get his tiercels to catch sage grouse in a stoop from a high pitch—that is, to come down and strike the grouse so hard that it's either mortally wounded and tumbles dead from the sky or falls to earth seriously injured. It can take years to train a bird to strike its quarry hard and hurt it rather than just strike a glancing blow and then follow it down into the brush. The instinct of the big female hybrid or gyrfalcon is to fly the grouse down—or chase it—and then catch it when it puts into the sagebrush and scrambles for cover. "Those big gyrfalcons don't even try to kill sage grouse on a stoop and will just grab them if they can," said Steve. "They know they can stay with them when they fly, so where's the sport in that?"

Over the decades, Steve's hunted sage grouse with jerkins (male gyrfalcons), female gyrfalcons, female hybrids, tiercel hybrids, and female peregrines. He's seen big birds killed when they hit sage grouse, so it isn't necessarily size but rather experience. "A bird isn't going to hurt itself if it knows what it's up against," he said. "I tell people who fly on ducks all the time that hitting a duck is just like hitting a giant marshmallow, and when they come up here and their bird hits a sage grouse, that's just like hitting a flying brick. And birds can kill themselves hitting a sage grouse because they're so much more dense." The only thing he hasn't flown on sage grouse are tiercel peregrines, because he thinks they're just a bit too small to do the job.

We finally made our way to an area near Rocky Flats where earlier in the week Steve had seen a large flock of grouse. As we drove along the two-track, the horizon got light, and then, very quickly, the sun rose above the Jack Morrow Hills, lighting the bottoms of some snow clouds that were off in the distance. There was a touch of wind, making the ten degrees feel even colder. Steve stopped the truck at the spot where he had seen the birds and went around back to let Tucker out. He opened Tucker's kennel, and before the dog jumped down from the tailgate, Steve put the shock collar and the telemetry around its neck. He also tied a fluorescent-orange vest around Tucker's neck so the mostly white dog would show up against the snow.

Tucker leaped from the truck and ran, working his way out into the field. He ran full speed—head forward, thin rope of a tail out, legs flying—dodging the two-foot-tall sagebrush bushes. Steve got back in the truck, and we moved slowly along the road, keeping Tucker in front of us. First he was to the right of the truck, then he crossed the road and worked the field to the left of us, running hundreds of yards in each direction.

"Oh, he's getting birdy," said Steve as Tucker slowed way down and ran several short passes in an area of sage to our left. "I really hope it's a hen because Jomo won't even fly at a big cock bird anymore." Steve threw the truck in park and went to the back to get Jomo. He stood there for a couple of minutes, placing the telemetry transmitters on Jomo's legs, and I sat in the warm cab for as long as possible. I knew from experience that Steve wanted me to stay in the cab until his bird was up in the air and could pin down the game.

A telemetry transmitter is a tiny device the weight of a quarter with a thin antenna about eight inches long; it emits a signal that can be picked up by a receiver that Steve carries with him. Like many falconers who fly birds in the West, Steve uses two transmitters on his birds—one on each leg—in case one of them quits working or falls off. In the early 1970s, before telemetry was developed for falconry, falconers used bells attached to the ankles of their birds as a way to keep track of where they were. When a bird with bells is flying, you can hear the wind ripping through the slots in the bells. Before telemetry, if you flew birds in the great open spaces of the West, every single time you went out, you risked losing your bird, particularly if it was a bird like a gyrfalcon, which can easily fly five miles in pursuit of prey. Telemetry really made hawking for sage grouse possible.

Steve brought Jomo around to the front of the truck. Tucker was on point about two hundred yards away—his body was as still as the body of a big dog full of energy could be, with a paw lifted and his tail straight up like a little flag. He began to creep forward just a step or two, which made Steve yell, "Whoa, Tucker. Whoa." And the dog stopped moving.

Steve loosened Jomo's hood with his teeth and his right hand and removed it. Jomo sat up, looked around, puffed out his feathers, took a crap, then pushed off Steve's outstretched, gloved left hand. He hung for just a moment in the wind, wings spread, then began to take slow, deliberate flaps. As he powered up into the sky, I opened my door as quietly as possible and came out to stand by Steve. The minute the slight breeze hit my face I was cold, even though I had on a winter coat, a hat pulled down over my ears, a scarf wrapped around my neck and pulled up to almost meet the hat, and thick gloves. I looked at Steve, who was standing there bareheaded and bare-handed (he had stashed his falconry glove in the game bag slung over his shoulder after Jomo took off). He was wearing his down vest over a couple of layers of shirts, and then his blue jeans over long underwear. He was completely absorbed in what was happening in the field and didn't seem to notice the weather.

"Where's my bird? Where's Jomo?" he yelled.

"He's way up at about three o'clock." I knew that sometimes Steve had a hard time seeing his bird because he was blind in one eye, so I answered, pointing to a little speck in the cold blue sky. Jomo was flying in tighter and tighter circles a thousand feet above the dog. "Is he in position? Is he behind me?" yelled Steve. "Yep," I said. "He's coming around." Steve started running toward the dog, who was still on point, and began waving his hands and yelling, *"Heeaahhh! Heeaahhh!"*

About fifteen dark football-shaped birds burst from the sagebrush in front of Tucker. I heard their wings whirring as they flew as fast as they could, away from the crazy man who was waving his arms. Sometimes sage grouse didn't even flush when Steve ran toward them because they were so wary of the falcon flying above them, but this morning, they all took off. As they flew Steve yelled, "Damn it! They're all big cock birds."

As the birds flushed, Jomo tucked his wings to his sides and began to plummet toward earth. He was at 1,000 feet . . . 800

feet . . . 600 feet . . . The falcon cut through the air like a hot knife through ice cream. When he got closer to the grouse he seemed to hesitate, but then he hit one of them with a glancing blow. The grouse dropped several feet, then righted itself and powered on. Jomo threw himself up into the air about a hundred feet, then came back down and gave chase to the grouse. Although the falcon was a faster bird, he had used some energy just hitting the grouse and then wheeling back up into the sky, so it looked like the grouse was going to win this morning. Jomo flew around a bit more while Steve ran through the sagebrush the grouse had burst from, hoping to kick up a straggler. No such luck. Steve pulled a sage grouse carcass from his game bag and reluctantly called Jomo down by throwing it up in the air. Jomo came down onto the carcass, then Steve picked him up and offered him a dead sparrow as a snack.

Steve was so disappointed with Jomo's performance that he didn't really want to talk about it. Maybe witnessing the effects of age on Jomo was hard to bear; after all, this falcon had been his steady hunting partner for much of his adult life. Maybe the world that had moments before seemed so big and full of possibilities had suddenly shrunk to a bird and his hesitation, to a tiny glimpse of the future. Maybe, as he saw Jomo's hesitation, he felt his own aching bones and muscles as he stood in the middle of a freezing cold Wyoming desert.

I wondered why Steve seemed to attach so much importance to Jomo's performance in the field. I mean, this bird had been flying hard for twenty seasons, and while captive falcons could certainly live that long, it was almost unheard-of for a bird who hunted as hard as Jomo did for six months out of each year to reach that age. Then I realized that Steve worked Jomo as hard as he worked himself. He'd anthropomorphized his bird and decided that Jomo—like himself—would not be happy sitting in a chamber being fed regularly and relaxing his way toward death. He imagined that the old bird would go out in a blaze of glory and be killed by a golden eagle after a spectacular flight in pursuit of a sage grouse five times his weight. He'd decided that those were the death terms Jomo would choose for himself, and it was up to him, the falconer, to honor them.

We drove to our next hawking spot, because we still had three birds to fly, and Steve said, "My goal is to go out there and repeatedly make my bird feel successful, and I sure did that with Jomo over the years. I can look at my journal and see times when I had an amazing number of flights in a row without having a screwup."

For Steve it's all about the challenge of the hunt. He loves the preparation and the amount of work that goes into making it all happen while also making it seem somewhat effortless. "Part of it is to make it look like I kind of know what I'm doing even though it's so difficult to do," he said. "It took me years and years to get to this point, and most falconers get really frustrated because it's so hard to be successful over and over again."

Every falconer I've been around eventually quotes some variation of Murphy's Law: everything that can go wrong, will go wrong. Every single time a bird leaves a falconer's fist, there are so many things that can go wrong. The falcon won't go up high enough, or the dog will flush the game before the bird is in position in the sky, or a prairie falcon will come out of nowhere and begin to harass the falcon. Or the bird might catch a thermal and go way up and spy some ducks over the hill and fly out of sight. And there are the moments of sheer terror, when a golden eagle suddenly appears while the bird's in the sky or is preoccupied by sitting on a kill. There are some things a falconer never wants to witness. But these are the variables, and some of the chances a falconer takes when he releases that bird from his care. He can't protect the bird from nature—or its nature—once it leaves the fist. He can only try to plan for all the possible things that could go wrong, and sometimes he has to stand by helplessly as they do.

"I think the unpredictability is what makes it so addictive. It's a hard thing to make happen time and time again. It's the same reason someone climbs that really tall or difficult mountain," said Steve. "Because it's a challenge. Every time you complete your mission you get an exhilaration of accomplishment. This happens every time you fly your falcon because every single time it's a difficult conquest and it focuses you. Probably in some respects it's an addiction because it can give you the same release. If you have anything on your mind—anything that's troubling you—the minute your falcon takes off you don't think about that anymore. If you had your heart broken, you can get out and fly your falcon, and for the time your bird is in the air, whatever was heavy on your mind is gone.

"I guess you could call it a vice," he added.

7

The Boy Falconer

WHEN STEVE CHINDGREN was a boy of seven or eight, he tried to dig a tunnel through his backyard. He made a hole big enough to crawl into and crouched in there and pretended he had a little underground hut. When he wasn't in the tunnel, he covered the entrance with boards. One day his older half brother, his mother's son from an earlier marriage, told him to crawl in there, and for some reason, Steve did. The next thing Steve knew, his brother was putting the boards back over the hole, then he covered them with dirt and stamped it down. Steve knew he couldn't get out because he was too little to push past the boards and the dirt. Then he heard his brother laugh and say, "You'll never get out. You just dug your own grave and they'll never find you. You're going to be in there until you die." As his brother walked away, Steve heard him say, "See ya." And as he lay in the dark, Steve remembers thinking, *Will he ever come back and let me out or will I die in here?*

A couple of years before that, Steve's brother had told him to sit on a red stool that he'd placed in front of a white wall in their house. "Now don't move," he said. "We're going to play a circus game." He took several steps back, then aimed a dart gun at Steve and started firing. Steve tried not to move or look at the needle-sharp darts that whizzed past his head and stuck into the wall behind him. "If you try to escape, I'll shoot you," warned his brother as he stopped to put more darts in his gun. Steve took a chance and bolted from the stool, running toward the door. The next thing he remembers is pulling a dart out of his eye.

And people wonder why Steve is so intense; why he always has to be the best at whatever he tries to do; why he pushes himself so hard that his body feels as if it's going to seize up if he has to take another step; why he has to have falcons that can hunt the most difficult game in North America at the most brutal time of year; why he chooses to spend half the year living away from his family in order to fly his falcons in the wide-open sagebrush desert of Wyoming.

When I'm out in the field with him he sometimes screams at me, "Where's my bird, *where's my bird?*" as he strains with his one good eye to locate a backlit silhouetted speck of a bird a thousand feet up in the blue, blue sky.

Steve grew up in Emigration Canyon, along the route Brigham Young took when he led the first Mormon pioneers into the Great Salt Lake Basin. At the mouth of the canyon is Hogle Zoo, where Steve presents his bird show. It is right across the highway from This Is the Place Park, commemorating the spot where more than a hundred and sixty years earlier Brigham Young stopped, swept his arm across the valley, and proclaimed, "This is the place."

On a hot day in July, it took us about twenty minutes to go six miles on the canyon road because the county had decided to put in a water line, which entailed digging up the road section by section. Until recently, everyone who lived in the canyon has relied on well water and their own septic systems. Now that the canyon has become popular and half-million-dollar homes are springing up in little developments off the canyon road, the water and sewer issue has become a big one.

Once you really get into the canyon where it's too narrow for much development, it hasn't changed that much since Steve grew up there in the 1950s and 1960s. There's still only one road snaking through the canyon. Ruth's Diner is still down on a wide spot near the canyon mouth, although the current owner's probably not as mean as Ruth was. In the 1950s, Ruth dragged a trolley car partway up the canyon, plopped it down, fired up the hot plate, and called it a diner. Since then, Ruth's Diner has been a local oddity and a fixture. She was famous for screaming at the customers as she stood there in her floral-print housedress with a cigarette hanging out of the corner of her mouth. Steve didn't like to go in there because she was so mean, but one time when he and his friends were about nine years old, they collected some pop bottles from along the road-side and took them to Ruth to redeem for a couple of pennies apiece. They really wanted a candy bar, and they had enough money for one, but it was a hot day and they were thirsty too. Ruth sold them the candy bar, and when they had the nerve to ask for water she yelled at them and said she wasn't going to dirty any glasses for a bunch of kids. A guy at the counter said, "Aw, come on, Ruth, give the kids a drink of water." She shot him a dirty look and brought out one glass, poured some water in it, and said they'd all have to share.

As we drove up the canyon, it narrowed, and soon large oak and maple trees hugged the road, casting dark and light green stippled shadows on the houses they partially obscured. There are two kinds of people who live in the canyon: new people, who want to live in nice houses within minutes of downtown Salt Lake City, and old-timers, who live there because they want to be away from it all. These two groups might one day find them-selves in conflict because their interests are different, but so far all of them just keep to themselves.

According to some, Emigration Canyon is a hot spot for UFO encounters, and at certain times of year it's the place to be, because that's when aliens are most likely to fly by. The canyon has been a hot spot for UFO activity for decades. When Steve was growing up in the canyon, one of his neighbors—a guy with a long, long beard—cranked out a newsletter, which he mimeographed in his basement, about his experience of being abducted by aliens. Steve spent a good twenty years looking at every tree, every leaf, every rock, every bird, and every animal in that canyon, and he's never seen a UFO—but he's not willing to say it can't happen.

Mary Jane (MJ) Chindgren, Steve's mother, has lived in the canyon since she and Steve's father, Roy, bought a cabin there in 1947. They had already bought a plot of land near Salt Lake for five hundred dollars—a special deal for World War II veterans—and all they had to do was build on it. MJ said they'd had the plans picked out for the cutest house but then they'd heard there was a place for sale in the canyon. They drove up to the place that had the house-for-sale sign out front, rang the doorbell, and said, "We'll take it!" The woman who'd opened the door laughed and said, "This isn't the place," and pointed up the road to the twelve-by-sixteen-foot rustic summer cabin built of cement and plywood. MJ and Roy bought the cabin and gave up the plot in the city.

MJ grew up in Salt Lake City, and for years she and her father had come to the canyon to fish. She couldn't believe that now she was actually going to live there. "My in-laws thought I was crazy," she said. They wondered why anyone would give up a nice lot in the city for a cabin in the canyon. But she and Roy knew what they wanted. And looking back, she wouldn't change her life in the canyon for anything.

Over the next couple of decades Roy built the current house around the original cabin, and today MJ's home is an attractive two-story red-colored wood house with cobblestones covering the first-floor exterior in the front. It's built smack up against the side of the hill; the kitchen and large, open dining room/living room are on the second floor, and the bedrooms are on the first. While the house was being built the family had crammed into the first floor, where Steve had a bedroom that was just big enough to hold a bed and a toy chest. ("There was a toy chest in there?" Steve asked his mother when she said that.) A little later, when the second story had been built but not finished, the kids had bedrooms upstairs, but there were no stairs, and so for a while, to get to their bedrooms they had to go outside and climb a ladder that was leaning against the side of the house and then crawl through a second-story window.

Today the bits of lawn that haven't been turned into gardens or water features are lush and green. A little waterfall drops into a koi pond set into an extensive rock garden on one side of the driveway, and just last year MJ had stone steps and a stone slab patio put in down by the creek that runs in front of the property. She can sit down there and watch birds like dippers and gold-finches that come to the running water. There's a large concrete patio to one side of the house out back and a smaller, shadier patio just off the kitchen. There are flower-filled pots everywhere.

The small backyard is defined by several large pine trees that Roy planted in the fifties. Beyond the pines, the hillside becomes a tangle of oak and maple. You can still see the small wooden shed on the side of the hill that was the first mews Steve and Roy built. This is where BBG, a white gyrfalcon Steve got from Alaska, first lived. Behind that are a few cinder blocks and boards—remnants of a larger mews where Steve first tried to create hybrid birds. He tried to cross a prairie falcon and a saker falcon before anyone else in North America had succeeded. He failed as well.

Although today MJ has some health problems—a slow-growing inoperable brain tumor that's messing up her balance, and some arthritis—she's an elegant woman in her mideighties with a shoulder-length brown bob. She moves gracefully, even with a cane. It's easy to see where Steve gets his athleticism. Two little dogs, a cinnamon-colored Chihuahua and some kind of fluffy black-and-white mixed breed, follow her everywhere; they have been her companions for a couple of years.

The Chindgrens loved the water. MJ told me she was the first woman in the state of Utah to water-ski. Someone had brought some water skis over from California in the 1940s—big wide things—and she couldn't wait to try them. Later, in her father's garage, Roy and MJ's father built a beautiful Chris-Craft boat from a kit. It was big enough to hold seven people and two dogs. When he was a teenager, Steve used to load up his Volkswagen van, strap his water skis on top, throw a tape of Neil Young into the eight-track, and drive off in search of a body of water. He'd hustle water-skiing rides by standing on a dock in one of the many Utah freshwater lakes and holding out his thumb. He'd offer five bucks to anyone who could make him fall—he said they could do anything but stop the boat. He got some great rides that way and didn't have to pay up very often.

The Chindgrens also loved the snow. Roy, another native of Salt Lake City, was an early Nordic skier. When Steve was a kid, there were sets of long skinny skis everywhere in the house and in the auto mechanic's garage that Roy owned. Roy ran a rope tow up the side of the canyon and created a ski area. He figured out how the mechanisms worked and then made everything himself. This wasn't his first rope tow; he'd actually created the first commercial ski area in the Salt Lake region. He was also a champion alpine jumper, and when the Winter Olympics came to Salt Lake City in 2002, his name was inscribed on a plaque to show the city's long involvement in winter sports. One of Steve's first jobs was working at Snowbird, the ski area just up and over the hill from his house. You could safely say that Steve got his athleticism from both sides of the family.

Roy and MJ divorced when Steve was eighteen. Roy later remarried, but his second wife died not too long ago, and for the past year Roy has lived with Kathy, Steve's sister, in a town about three hours from Salt Lake.

As we sat on the stone slabs near the creek, trying to catch what little breeze there was on the sweltering midsummer day, we chatted about Steve's childhood, and it became clear that

MJ didn't have any idea of the cruelty Steve had endured at the hands of his half brother. Or if she did, she didn't want to talk about it. She told me that her other son had the same kind of passion for sport fishing that Steve had for falconry. "My other boy's about like Steve, but he fishes," she said. "He goes to Hawaii with me, and the kids follow him around like the Pied Piper. He has very quick reflexes and never loses a fish while the people all around him aren't getting any fish. It's just kind of amazing. I guess he got that athletic gene too."

On Steve's fiftieth birthday, he did three backflips in the air. Not back handsprings, but full somersaults in the air. He has it on videotape in case anyone doesn't believe him. On his sixtieth birthday, he wants to travel fifty feet while doing a handstand on a skateboard. He's wiry and strong, and he expects to be able to do whatever he wants with his body. But his body has other ideas. One time when I was visiting, he had to go to the bus station early in the morning to pick up a load of two thousand dead chicks packed in dry ice to feed the birds at the zoo. When he got there, the chicks were in three large boxes, which of course he picked up and loaded into his truck himself. Then we heard about it for the rest of the day. "I shouldn't have done that," he said as he held his lower back and paced around. But he wouldn't have thought of not doing it, because the job needed to be done, and, well, who else was going to do it?

Steve can run full speed better than any fifty-six-year-old I've ever seen. It's almost a Tom Cruise or Mel Gibson or Russell Crowe full-out run, with the legs moving so fast they make the man look like a cartoon character. But when Steve is running, it's to get to a bird that's down on a kill or to try to find a bird that's tail chasing a grouse. Every time I watch him power across a sagebrush-strewn desert in pursuit of a bird, I think, *Now, how does he do that?* And I always think of that endurance-training technique in which a young Indian brave was sent running through the desert holding a mouthful of water that he couldn't swallow. I bet if Steve had known about that as a teenager, he would have done it.

Instead, he hiked and skied and water-skied and rock-climbed and drove motorcycles really fast. When he was growing up, he knew every inch of Emigration Canyon. He hiked up and down every gully looking for birds. He made his own map of the canyon and named all the gullies and little ridges, and he placed marks on the map where he'd found hawk nests. Once when he was hiking up above his house he came across a field strewn with rusting baby buggies—skeletal metal frames with big metal wheels. It looked like a freaky baby-buggy graveyard. He figured they had been dumped there by a wagon whose driver had thought he could take a shortcut across the ridge and then dip down into the canyon rather than follow the Mormon Trail down through the center of the canyon. In Steve's wanderings he found metal rims from nineteenth-century wagons and little wooden wedges that pioneers had used to fix their wheels. He found the wedges at the place where the Donner party had spent a critical three weeks while they cleared a major rock obstruction from the trail. Not a good decision, in hindsight.

The canyon was Steve's playground, and he had the run of the place. When he was just a boy, he and his friend Jim decided they wanted to try to live off the land, so they headed out with backpacks and spears, which they were going to use to spear fish. Steve discovered it was easier to catch them with his hands than to use the spear. His mother knew they'd come back when they got hungry enough, and they did.

MJ took a real hands-off approach to child-rearing with Steve. I think she was also curious about just where the boundaries were going to be with him. When Steve was three, he climbed up onto a high dive and said he was going to jump off. MJ got in the water right under the diving board and said she'd get him, although she thought he'd probably get to the end, take one look, and decide to go back down the way he'd come up. But he didn't. He jumped. With everything he did later on, like climbing cliffs to reach nests so he could photograph birds, she felt like she couldn't say no to him. She felt he was going to do dangerous things whether she wanted him to or not. She said she had to become detached or it would have driven her crazy.

One thing MJ did encourage him to do was judo. When Steve was about eleven, Steve and his mother went to a flower show at the Buddhist temple in Salt Lake and saw a judo demonstration. Steve was completely mesmerized. He started learning judo, and within a couple of years he went to Denver and won the national championship trophy for his age and weight class. "There's something about men that do judo," said MJ. "They have a confidence and they don't get into confrontations because they're secure with themselves. They just have a thing about them that makes people think they don't want to fool with them, but it's not threatening." Doing judo honed Steve's reflexes and taught him how to fall properly, which became useful when climbing trees and cliffs to check on birds' nests.

Ultimately, when it came down to birds versus skiing or judo or water-skiing, there was no contest. It was always birds, and these other activities were mere distractions. From the time Steve was about eight, he had a bird. His favorite movies and television shows were things like *Lassie* and Mutual of Omaha's *Wild Kingdom*. His parents weren't interested in nature at all.

After his first sighting of a Cooper's hawk, the one he'd seen in his backyard and then drawn by modifying his *Tyrannosaurus rex* picture, he was consumed by dreams of hawks and wanted to get one. He already had a menagerie of turtles and snakes and whatever else he could find in the canyon. First it was pigeons (he took over his brother's pigeons when his brother didn't want them), then magpies, and a little later it was kestrels, red-tailed hawks, Cooper's hawks—anything he could take from a nest or capture. Right after he saw his first Cooper's hawk, his mother helped him find the entry for *hawks* in the encyclopedia. That entry said *See falconry,* and when Steve saw the photograph of the man holding the falcon on his fist, he was hooked. He became obsessed with the idea of falconry. He found a book in the school library that had pictures of hawks and falcons in it, and he carried it back and forth to school for three years so he could stare at the pictures during his free time at school and, better yet, try to draw them.

On weekends Steve would hitch a ride down the canyon with his father, who owned an auto mechanic's garage across town. He'd get off at the zoo, which was at the mouth of the canyon and was free, and would spend the day watching the birds of prey. It didn't take long before the zoo director noticed this young boy hanging around the raptor cages. He told Steve that when he got bigger, the zoo director would let him take one of the hawks home and care for it, and that he would give him a call if a small hawk was brought in. The director invited Steve into his office, which contained a large terrarium holding a rubber boa snake. Steve told the director he saw lots of those in the canyon and could get him another one. That was the beginning of a relationship that would last for years—Steve supplied the zoo with snakes and scorpions, and the zoo director let him hang around the hawks and falcons and eagles.

One day the zoo director called Steve at home and said he had a bird for him. A small sparrow hawk (which is what they used to call a kestrel) had been brought to the zoo. This was the late 1950s, and there were no real rules about who could own what. Steve didn't know about jesses yet, so he kept the kestrel in a cage in his room. He didn't dare let the bird fly outside because he didn't want it to fly away, but he let it fly free in the house. They played hide-and-seek, with Steve hiding and the bird finding him. Steve didn't know how to care for a raptor, so he fed it a diet of beef heart, and eventually the bird developed some nutritional deficiencies and died.

Years later, Steve was working the rope tow at the little ski area on the mountain and listening to music on the radio; when the news came on, the announcer said that the zoo director had been bitten by a puff adder—it had sunk one fang in his finger—and had died. "He basically got me started in falconry, and it always feels a little weird that I'm doing a bird show at the same zoo today," said Steve.

The bird that had the most impact on Steve when he was a young boy was a big red-tailed hawk he named Shoulders. He got Shoulders when he saw an ad in the local paper—*Found Hawk, Liberty Park*—and begged his mother to take him to see the bird. Shoulders was a big immature red-tail with a leather strap around one leg. Steve told the guy he wanted the hawk if no one claimed him. The guy said Steve could have him if he paid for the cost of the ad, and MJ paid it. Steve was only eight years old at the time. That bird went everywhere with Steve as he explored the hills around his house; he named him Shoulders because the bird always sat on his shoulder.

Steve and Shoulders spent a lot of time walking up gullies and over ridges. It wasn't unusual for Shoulders to fly away from Steve and land in a big tree. Steve would climb the tree and try to entice the hawk to him with bits of food; other times, Steve would climb the tree and sit there with his bird. He wanted to know what it was like to be a hawk. He wanted to see what a hawk saw from a high perch. And of course, what he really wanted was to push off from a tree limb and take to the air, like Shoulders. Sitting high in a tree with the wind in his face and his hawk next to him was, he thought, as good as it got.

Steve and Shoulders were inseparable. They were like a kid and his dog. Steve got to watch his hawk hunt every day and became fascinated with the variety of prey—from snakes to rabbits—the red-tail went after.

He kept the hawk tied with a tiny chain to a perch in the backyard, but Shoulders was always getting loose. One day, shortly before Christmas, Steve watched as Shoulders broke free from the perch and flew away. The bird caught a thermal and soared up and over the mountain behind the house and was gone. "When you're that age and see your hawk go over a mountain, you know it's gone," said Steve. "I just dropped down to the ground and cried."

He walked around for days whistling for Shoulders and carrying raw meat in the little leather transistor radio case he used as a hawking bag. He was so depressed, he couldn't think of anything else. Finally he took his sleeping bag and hiked up the mountain to look for the bird. He decided he was going to stay there until he had Shoulders back. Although the family wasn't religious, when he reached the summit he dropped to his knees and prayed to God for the return of his hawk. After several hours he got really cold and dragged himself back down the mountain.

"I was a really emotional kid about that hawk," said Steve. "I remember lying there in bed on Christmas morning and not wanting to get up because I didn't care about anything. My mom asked if I was going to open my presents. I said maybe in a while. 'Well,' she said, 'you oughtta go look in that tree at the end of the yard.' I leaped up and there he was, and when he saw me he flew down to me.

"I loved that bird," he added. "I used to sing to him as we walked through the mountains."

Around this time Steve saw a copy of Frederick II's *The Art of Falconry* in a bookstore in Salt Lake City. He knew he had to have it because it was about falconry, but it cost twenty dollars. So he picked apricots from his grandmother's trees, placed them in a wagon, and started going around the neighborhood selling the fruit. When people asked what he was going to do with the money, he said he was going to buy a book, and that always clinched the sale. Steve still keeps this copy of what he calls "King Frederick's book" in a glass-fronted bookcase in the cabin.

There's a large framed color photograph of Steve at a 1968 Utah falconry meet hanging in the basement—what I call the bunkhouse—of the cabin. He would have been seventeen at the time. He's extremely handsome, with blond collar-length hair, dark eyebrows, and strong features. He's wearing a tan field coat with a brown corduroy collar and cuffs over a dark brown turtleneck. You can see the strap from a leather game bag slung over his shoulder, bandolier style. His right hand is jammed into his jacket pocket. Perched on his outstretched, gloved left hand is a hooded female prairie falcon with a dark brown back and streaks of brown stretching down the white of her front. Behind Steve are snow-covered mountains and a blue Utah sky. His lips are drawn into an ever-so-slight smile, and everything about the picture—the bird, the mountains, the handsome boy, the comfortable stance—screams self-confidence. Everything except the eyes. There's something about the eyes looking directly into the camera and not smiling that makes Steve seem vulnerable.

Around the same time that this photograph was taken, Steve was working at Snowbird, a ski area just over the top of the canyon. He worked nights and weekends, and, like everything he did, he worked harder and longer than anyone else on the crew. He had to be the best. He spotted a golden eagle's nest on a cliff face across from the lodge, and he decided he wanted to rappel down to the nest, get behind the young birds that were in there, and take a photograph of the lodge, creating a kind of eagle's-eye view of the ski area. By this time he was seriously into photography, partially because it was a way to justify peering into every raptor nest he found.

One day before work, he got his camera, a two-way radio, and two of the longest ropes he could find, and he hiked around to the top of the cliff. A friend of his stayed by the lodge with binoculars and the other radio so he could guide him down to the nest. Steve tied off the rope around a sturdy tree on top of the cliff and headed down. He got to the end of the first rope, tied on the second one, and kept going. On an overhang, he started swinging to push himself out and away from the cliff face so he could look for the nest. All of a sudden, rocks came raining down on him. He panicked and took his brake hand to cover his head—one rock hit him pretty good—and when he let go, the carabiner started sliding down the rope. He squeezed the rope with his other hand until he wore a bloody groove into the palm. When he finally stopped, he was near the end of the second rope and still a couple of hundred feet above the ground.

"Talk about everything you're not supposed to do," he said. It took him eight hours to climb back up the rope. He tied off and let his arms rest, then got up his energy and started climbing again. He dropped the radio early on. Eventually he felt so weak that he thought he was going to die. He took everything off that had any weight to it and tossed it. His Nikon camera was the last thing to go.

When he finally climbed up over the edge of the cliff and reached solid ground, he just sat there feeling the sensation of flat ground and marveling at how nice it was. He was a bloody mess—the rock that hit him had cut his head, and his hands were shredded—so he was glad to be alive.

When he got home he didn't tell his mother what had really happened—he told her the palms of his hands looked like raw hamburger because he'd gotten rope burns at work. Not long after that, MJ went up to Snowbird to have a bite to eat with Steve on his lunch break. She saw a kid in the parking lot who said, "Boy, Mrs. Chindgren, I bet you were sure worried about Steve," and she didn't know what he was talking about.

"'He just about got killed,' the kid said. 'Didn't he tell you?' And I felt bad because I didn't know," MJ said. "I'd just thought it was some sort of rope burn from work."

8

Searching for Falcons

STEVE GOT MORE INVOLVED in falconry as a teenager, flying several different species of birds, including Cooper's hawks; kestrels; his red-tail, Shoulders, of course, which he had into his teen years; and finally a prairie falcon. As he spent more time out in the fields with his birds, he noticed—and came to be noticed by— the small community of falconers around Salt Lake in the 1960s. He became good friends with Terry, another falconer, who was just a couple of years older than Steve, and they decided they were going to try to trap some peregrines up north. Terry had a Volkswagen Beetle and Steve had $150, and they were prepared to go all the way to Alaska if necessary in order to get some birds.

Steve had just graduated from high school and was working as a truck driver at a produce company. He saved all his money, and that fall he and Terry piled into the VW and headed north. They had traps and trapping gear and took the spare tire out to make room for a cage of pigeons to use during trapping. Terry had a hooded sharp-shinned hawk sitting in the back seat of the car. They camped along the way and used a little Coleman stove to heat up cans of soup. This was a budget trip because Terry hadn't brought any money with him—he had the car—and Steve had brought only enough money to cover food and gas for a week or two.

They didn't see any peregrines in Idaho or Montana or Canada so they pushed north. Although they crossed into Canada and then back into the United States, no one said anything about the hooded sharp-shin riding in the back seat. By the time they got to Alaska they were low on money and a little desperate for food and were trying to run over rabbits to cook up on the Coleman stove. Terry had a .22 with him because he was a fanatic about making sure his sharp-shin had fresh small birds to eat every day. Steve was just itching to find a peregrine. "We spent so darn much time trying to shoot little birds for the hawk that I never thought we'd have time to trap anything," said Steve.

They made it to Eagle, Alaska, a spot along the Yukon River, where they set up camp and tried their hand at trapping. They hiked out to the river and set up a lure trap using the pigeons they'd brought from Utah, and they sat there all day for two long days flashing pigeons on a pole. Only ravens came by to check them out. Disappointed, they packed up and headed south to Homer, Alaska; they were surprised that they hadn't seen a single peregrine so far on the trip. Terry decided they should call an ornithologist they knew who studied Alaskan peregrines and ask him where they should look. Although he gave them some advice about where to look during the hundred-and-fifty-dollar phone call (falconers like to talk about birds; fortunately, they had MJ's credit card), the boys came up short and decided it was too cold and too late in the season to find peregrines, so they left Alaska without a bird.

By the time they left, they were living on broth cubes and water and, as Steve put it, "were getting really scurvy." Steve was trying to eat any vegetation he thought was edible and got sick with a terrible case of dysentery. They didn't have a lot of clothes with them because they hadn't planned on being gone long, and they were starting to look really grubby because they hadn't bathed or shaved. And Steve was ripping pieces off a long-sleeved purple turtleneck he wore to wipe his butt, which was in pretty bad shape.

"So here we were. I have my whole belly hanging out of my ripped shirt and we didn't really have any money and we're trying to get back and are driving in shifts and I'm on the night shift. I fell asleep and we went off the road," said Steve. "Fortunately it didn't happen somewhere where there was a cliff and a lake, and we ended up just going through a bunch of small trees. I know it did something to the wheel, though, because after that the car shimmied really bad and would only smooth out if you got going about eighty miles per hour.

"We're continuing on and we're in Montana and I'm trying to go the speed limit but I don't know what the speed limit is. A car comes up behind me and I go faster and pretty soon I'm going eighty and it turns out to be a police car and the lights start flashing and it pulls me over. And I'm thinking, *Oh, shit*, because we barely had enough money for gas to get home. My mom had wired money to Anchorage for food and gas and we pigged out at a Kentucky Fried Chicken place and used up all the food money so at that point we had just enough money for gas and no extra money for food.

"This officer who pulled me over said I had to pay the money for the fine right there on the spot and I told him I couldn't do that because then we wouldn't be able to get home. He said I was going to jail. So he took me to a little old house and took my belt and wallet and coat and put me in a little cell in the basement of this old building. It was late September and there was one little window to the outside that had bars on it but no glass.

"It got down close to zero that night, and there I was wearing that ripped-up purple shirt with my belly hanging out. The room had rock walls, one light bulb turned on, a toilet with no seat, and nothing to wash with or anything. There were these little cages they used to put prisoners in along the back wall and then there were some thin cotton blue-and-white mattresses and some old green army blankets covered with puke. And it just reeked. So I'm walking around this place and I went and pounded on the wooden doors and asked for my coat. He said, *You got blankets,* and slammed the door. So I had to pull the pukey blankets up over me and try to go to sleep."

Terry spent the night driving around in the VW while Steve served his time for speeding. The next morning when they let Steve out, Terry said, "Boy, are you lucky. You got to spend the night in a nice warm jail and I had to drive around all night with the heater on because it was freezing." And Steve thought, *If you only knew . . .*

Steve and Terry made it all the way back to Salt Lake City and didn't see a single peregrine. They knew by then that the birds had migrated south, and because they had put in so much time and effort they decided to keep going. They ditched the car, raided their bank accounts, and sold some belongings to scrape together funds for a quick expedition. They had had enough adventure on their trip north, so this time they brought along enough money that they wouldn't have to worry about where they were going to stay and what they were going to eat. They bought two plane tickets to Corpus Christi, Texas, where they planned to rent a car and head to Padre Island to try to trap some birds.

In the 1960s, if you were a falconer looking for peregrines, Padre Island was the place to go. Tundra peregrines migrating from the Arctic to South America along the central flyway, a major migratory route, stopped at Padre Island—a long barrier island off the east coast of Texas—before heading across the Gulf of Mexico. They sat on the dunes, on pieces of driftwood, on anything that put them above the sand. And these birds were hungry. A falconer could go out and flash a pigeon, and a peregrine would be on it immediately. Steve and Terry knew about the falcons at Padre, and they also knew that state game wardens had Padre on their radar screen and were starting to crack down on falconers who came to trap birds. Although peregrines had not been listed as endangered—the Endangered Species Act wouldn't come into being until 1972—state game wardens would arrest any falconer they caught trying to trap a bird on the beach.

Terry knew he could spend only two days in Texas before he'd get fired from his job. As it was, he had to lie and tell his boss that someone had died. Terry and Steve rented a Ford Pinto in Corpus and drove to a feed store, where they found a guy who would sell them some pigeons. With the pigeons, they drove to Padre. At this point, Steve and Terry were getting on each other's nerves and were frustrated because they had driven all over hell's half acre and didn't have anything to show for their efforts. They drove out onto the beach, got a pigeon set on a trap, and—*boom!*—a beautiful tundra peregrine came right down on the flapping pigeon. They slipped a hood on the bird and took the falcon to the motel where they were going to stay the night. Then they had to decide who would keep the falcon. Steve thought the only fair thing to do was flip a coin, and Terry agreed. Steve won the toss.

"Terry was so upset because at that point he didn't think he was going to get a falcon and here I had this great bird. The first time I unhooded it, it just sat on my hand and pumped its wings— it didn't even try to fly! And it was just the most beautiful thing I'd ever seen," said Steve. "We fed it and I hooded it and set it in the bathroom and told Terry we'd get out in the morning and get him one. There was a lot of tension in the room at that point because he wanted that bird really bad. We ended up getting in a fistfight in the motel room. After we fought we were friends again."

The next morning they went out to the beach again and tried to look inconspicuous as they searched for peregrines. They saw one sitting on a dune and trapped it, but then a guy came running over the dune yelling, "Hey, that's my bird!" He was another falconer and he'd thought Steve and Terry were the game wardens, so he'd hidden when the car drove up. They gave the guy the bird, and then he helped them trap a bird for Terry.

They bought little gym bags to carry the birds home in.

They hooded the birds, wrapped them, taped their feet, and put them in the bags with their clothes. This was before the airlines hand-checked everything that was carried onto the plane. They had a layover in Denver and stayed in a hotel, and that night they got out some leather they'd brought with them and made some jesses for the birds. The next morning they wrapped and hooded the birds again and were on their way out when Steve noticed his scissors sitting on top of the television, so he stuck them in the bottom of the gym bag, beneath his falcon. They were just starting to put metal detectors in airports, but Steve and Terry didn't know that.

"So we're getting ready to go on the plane and Terry walks by and it was fine and all of a sudden the machine goes *beep beep beep beep* and the guy asks me, 'What's in the bag?' I say, 'I've got my trained falcon in here.' 'Falcon? Let me see it.' He takes a look at it and wants to know if the airline knows I've got the bird. 'Oh, yeah,' I say. 'I fly with it all the time.' He never did look for the scissors. He asks if I've got a permit for the bird so I whip out my state falconry license and he lets me go through.

"So I sit down next to Terry and all of a sudden there are two guys in suits walking down the aisle of the plane with the guy from the metal detector and they're looking straight at me. And Terry's pushing his bag under the seat and pretending not to know me. They say, 'Come with us, son, and bring that bird.' So Terry's thinking he's in big trouble and is just trying to disappear. So I get my bag and follow them and we get right up to the front and the pilot comes out of the cockpit and asks what the problem is. 'This guy's got a falcon in his bag and the airline wasn't aware that he had it,' says the man from the metal detector. 'Falcon! You a falconer? I've always been fascinated with falconry,' says the pilot. 'Let me look at it.' And the other guys just stand there because he's the pilot of the plane. The pilot asks why the falcon can't be on the plane. And they say the airline says it might be a risk to other passengers if it gets loose. The pilot says, 'Looks safe to me. I'll set it up here in the cockpit with me. Let's go.' So he takes the bag and gives it back to me in Salt Lake.

"We were always environmentalists," said Steve. "We thought we'd enhance these birds' chances of surviving by flying them for a season. They flew so great and it's actually amazing we didn't lose them because we didn't have telemetry back in those days. In the spring we took them out to the Farmington Bay Bird Refuge and let them go.

"Those were the only peregrines I ever trapped. I was glad we got in on the tail end of what used to be an annual thing for American falconers. Most of the guys who did all the trapping down there in the early sixties are dead now," said Steve. "I'd trap a peregrine in a second if it became legal again."

Steve returned to Padre Island the following autumn to try to trap another peregrine, only this time he took his girlfriend. They headed out in an old VW bus with a rebuilt engine but something went wrong and the engine seized in Las Cruces, New Mexico. They made their way to a gas station and the attendant said he'd tow them to the VW dealer for twenty dollars, so he attached the van to his truck with a tow strap and they careened down the freeway going about sixty-five miles an hour. Steve and his girlfriend eventually made it to the Gulf Coast of Texas, and from there they traveled up to Louisiana, driving on all the beaches and keeping a lookout for birds. They didn't see any peregrines and so they decided to try their luck on Padre Island.

State game wardens pulled them over the minute they got on the island, and when they asked Steve and his girlfriend what they were doing there, Steve said they were bird watching. The game wardens got their permission to search the van. First the wardens found the pigeons Steve had been planning to use for trapping; the wardens asked what the pigeons were for. Steve said it was none of their business. Next the game wardens found a snare. Then a trapping vest.

They started writing tickets. The game wardens said that since Steve and his girlfriend had trapping paraphernalia, they were being given a citation for attempting to trap a peregrine. Steve, who can pick a nit better than most, said, "How can I attempt to trap something I haven't even seen?" The wardens said that would be up to the judge. "But we haven't done anything wrong," said Steve. "Maybe we decided not to trap any because we haven't seen them and have decided they're getting rare."

That afternoon Steve and his girlfriend went to the courthouse in Port Isabella, but before they got inside, the arresting officer pulled Steve aside and said, "Mr. Chindgren, this is how we play the game. You go in there and plead not guilty and we're going to be charging you and your little girlfriend with attempting to trap peregrine falcons and while awaiting a court date you and your little girlfriend are going to be in our Port Isabella jail, and your little girlfriend ain't gonna like it very much. She ever been in jail before? Well, I can tell you it's not a very nice place to be, but it's up to you. But if you plead guilty, we won't charge your girlfriend and you pay a thirty-five-dollar fine and you get the hell out of town." So Steve thought it over and in the end decided he couldn't see her going to jail.

This old justice of the peace came into the courtroom wearing a pair of overalls and said, "What's it gonna be? Guilty or not guilty for attempting to trap a peregrine falcon?" Steve said, "Well, I guess if you can be guilty of attempting to trap something you haven't even seen, I guess it's guilty," and the justice said, "Guilty. Them peregrine falcons are as American as a bald eagle; they got a fistful of arrows in one foot and an olive branch in the other." Before Steve and his girlfriend left the courthouse, the judge took the trapping vest and hung it on the wall behind his desk, alongside a jar of pot, a switchblade, and a sawed-off shotgun.

Steve went back home and trapped a passage prairie falcon— a passage bird is a bird on migration—and flew that bird for the season. But he had been reading Frederick II's *The Art of Fal-*

conry, and Frederick extolled the virtues of flying a gyrfalcon—the largest falcon in the world—so pretty soon that was all Steve could think about. He also took Frederick's advice to heart. Frederick wrote, "For, as the cultivation of an art [falconry] is long and new methods are constantly introduced, a man should never desist in his efforts but persist in its practice while he lives, so that he may bring the art itself nearer to perfection." Flying a gyrfalcon was another step in his quest for perfection.

Steve knew he'd have to get back up to Alaska to trap a gyrfalcon because these were birds of the Arctic. He also knew that what he was about to do was illegal because you couldn't bring a gyrfalcon into the States from Canada. But he thought of it in terms of being only borderline illegal: it was legal to trap and to fly a gyrfalcon in Utah at that time, but gyrfalcons rarely came into Utah. Another piece of advice from Frederick rolled around in his head: "[The falconer] must possess marked sagacity; for, though he may, through the teachings of experts, become familiar with all the requirements involved in the whole art of falconry, he will still have to use all his natural ingenuity in devising means of meeting emergencies."

This was 1970, and the line between legal and illegal was extremely squishy, particularly to young people. The Vietnam War—a war many considered illegal at the time—was raging half a world away, and almost everyone knew someone who was over there. It's not the same as today, when military service is voluntary and the people who end up in conflicts are there because they've enlisted. Back then, someone ended up in Vietnam because his number came up and he got drafted by the government and his only choice was go to war or defy the government and leave the country. At the same time, a cultural revolution was taking place. Hair got longer, skirts got shorter, and drugs and sex were flowing. There was a sense of uncertainty about the near future. Young people were in a rebellious mood; the mentality was "us versus them." If parents and the older generation did it, the young people did the opposite. They hated their parents' music, clothes, hair. Their parents hated their music, their clothes, their hair. The parents didn't understand the kids. The kids didn't understand the parents. College campuses erupted with student demonstrations, and people took to the streets to protest what they felt was an unjustified, secretive war. The year 1968 saw the murders of Bobby Kennedy and Martin Luther King Jr., and it felt as if the world were going crazy. That generation lived for the moment because they didn't know what the hell was going to happen in the future. It felt simultaneously freeing and nihilistic.

This same rebellious spirit and feeling of mistrust took hold in many of the younger falconers. For years, they had seen older falconers flying peregrines that had been trapped at Padre Island, and now, when the young people tried to trap their own birds, they were hauled off to jail. And the authorities began to view falconers with suspicion, because falconry wasn't a popular or well-understood sport. Although in many states it was still legal to shoot birds of prey, in several it was illegal to take a bird to use for falconry. It made no sense to someone who saw himself as doing what was best for the bird, someone who believed he was enhancing the bird's chance of survival by getting it through that critical first year—a time when as many as 90 percent of the young birds die.

Falconers who came of age in the late 1960s always felt as if they had been born a year or two too late. They missed the great years on Padre, when the birds were there for the taking. They felt hassled and harassed by cops and game wardens wherever they went, and many of them began to fly under the radar. The members of the legal system couldn't imagine why people would do this if they weren't making big money from it—they couldn't understand that falconers just wanted to be left alone to fly their birds. When falconry regulations were enacted, in the early 1970s, some falconers said, *Screw that,* and just continued to fly birds until they got caught. Others did what they had to do to be legal, but they didn't like it and always suspected the authorities were gearing up to make the sport illegal. A dozen years later, the federal government went after falconers they believed were illegally selling birds to the Arabs. To this day, falconers of Steve's generation feel persecuted and paranoid. In this context, Steve's actions may have been illegal, but, in his mind at least, they were not wrong. In his opinion, he was helping these birds survive. He did his best to avoid the authorities that were monitoring falconry. He believed they were getting out of control.

Steve would do almost anything to get a gyrfalcon, but he didn't want to end up in jail for it. He knew this trip north was going to take some advance planning. He flew to Fort Collins, Colorado, to attend a raptor research conference so he could find out more about gyrfalcons. He learned that these birds were most numerous in western Alaska, on the Seward Peninsula and north of it, along the Noatak River. A friend of his from Snowbird, the ski area where he had worked as a teenager, wanted to go along because he thought it would be a cool trip. Steve told him that the trip could be a "one-way deal" because he was going to the Arctic to get a gyrfalcon and wasn't coming back until he had one. The friend went along anyway.

The last time Steve had gone to Alaska, there hadn't been a border check going into the state from Canada. This time, there was. Although Steve had hidden all his trapping gear, the border inspector noticed a picture of a prairie falcon Steve had taped to the wall of the VW bus and asked if he was a falconer. To Steve, it sounded like the guard was asking, *Are you a bank robber?* The border guard motioned the bus over and proceeded to tear it apart. He found an old falconry hood under the seat, which he picked up with a pencil, and told Steve to come into the office while he called the U.S. Fish and Wildlife Service. He told Fish and Wildlife he had two falconers entering the state who were probably looking for birds. Then he called Alaska Fish and Game, at which point Steve started thinking he was screwed but then realized they hadn't done anything wrong, so they couldn't be denied entry into the state.

Steve knew he needed to be sneaky. He and his friend hid the van in a postal service parking lot near the airport in Anchorage and then walked to the airport carrying their backpacks. They bought tickets for a commercial airline flight that took people on tours of the Arctic. The tour's first stop was Kotzebue, which was across the bay from the mouth of the Noatak River. Steve was excited that he might actually get to the Noatak, but when they got there, he realized there was no way they could get across the bay, which looked more like an ocean. They hopped back on the plane and went to the next stop, Nome. There they talked to an old-timer and told him they were looking for gyrfalcons to photograph, and he told them the birds were around. So Steve and his friend started walking out the Nome-Teller Highway, which was nothing more than a dirt road cut into the tundra, heading toward the Eskimo village of Teller, about seventy miles away.

Both Steve and his friend had guns; Steve had a .22 to shoot game for his bird when he got it, and his friend had a bigger gun because he was afraid of bears. The old-timer had told them, "You don't want to go poking around there this time of year because the mosquitoes got those bears ornery and you get down in them willows and you gonna get ate," so Steve's friend was scared to death. They hiked all day, and finally heard a flatbed pickup truck coming along. The driver stopped and asked them what the hell they were doing out there. Steve told him they were doing some photography and were looking for snowy owls and falcons. The driver told them there were gyrfalcons around and that a couple of years ago some Arabs had come looking for gyrfalcons and found some. He told them to hop in and he'd give them some dinner.

The driver's name was Chuck, and he had a fluoride mine just past the little river called Cripple Creek. He was the only person who lived out there. He had bad freeze burns all over his face from frostbite that he'd gotten when he and his wife—an Eskimo woman—had tried to make it into Nome on snowmobiles. The weather had gotten so bad that he'd told her to stay under a bridge while he went ahead to get the supplies. By the time he got back, she had frozen to death. He had two kids— Charlie and Chicken—and they had a pet raven and a dog that was half wolf and half malamute. Steve and his friend stayed with Chuck for a couple of days; he told them he'd seen gyrfalcons down by Cripple Creek, and they could probably hike up the creek and find a nest.

Chuck also told them about some old miners' cabins near the river that they could stay in. These cabins had been there since the gold-mining days. They picked one that was full of furniture and had most of the windows still intact and used it as a base camp. It was summer, so there were twenty-four hours of daylight up near the Arctic Circle. Steve hiked along Cripple Creek every day, looking for gyrfalcon nests, while his friend stayed at the cabin. The friend was getting nervous because they had been in Alaska for a while, and he'd started to think Steve had meant it when he'd said it could be a one-way trip. At night, the two of them would sit around the camp and Steve would say things like "I wonder how long we can make it through the winter." And although they were shooting game, such as ptarmigan, and had plenty to eat, the friend was really worried; at that point, they had been gone for a couple of weeks, and it seemed like there was a good possibility they would never make it home.

Finally, though, Steve found an eyrie on Cripple Creek that had three chicks. He took one out of the nest and brought it back to the cabin. It was a big downy chick, about twenty-three days old. Now came the tough part—getting the bird back to the States. Steve shot ptarmigan for it, and every time it ate or saw

Steve it would scream, *Gack gack gack gack,* and Steve thought, *If this happens in the airport, we're going to be in big trouble.*

Steve took some willow branches and duct tape and made a hidden pocket in his backpack—a nook just big enough to hide the chick. Chuck had told them when and where to meet him if they ever wanted to go to town, so they packed up their belongings and hiked to the road on the appointed day and time, and when Chuck stopped, they jumped onto the back of the flatbed and rode to the airport. Once there, they had to wait quite a while, and there were lots of tourists around. Steve, who looked like a modern-day mountain man at that point because he hadn't been able to shave or clean up in weeks, took out a big knife and a stick and began to whittle, which kept people away from him and his backpack. He gave the bird a lot of food to make sure it was full and hoped it was getting somewhat tame and wouldn't scream as much when it saw him.

"I had to check my backpack as luggage because it was so big," said Steve. "So they take it away and we're on the plane getting ready to take off and all of a sudden I hear an explosion and I see fire on the wing. They shut down the engines, and people are jumping out of their seats, and the plane goes right to the end of the runway and rolls off the edge and I think we're going to crash but we don't. They evacuate everyone off the plane in a hurry. So here I am in the airport and the plane's stuck out there on the end of the runway with my bird in the cargo hold. They said they were going to put us on another plane and get that one fixed and that they would send all the luggage on to Anchorage and people could pick it up there. I was totally panicked and pacing around the airport, trying to figure out what to do. Finally I went up to the guy and said, 'Sorry, sir, but I didn't take my insulin shot before we left and I can't wait three hours for my shot. I'm a diabetic.' So they got my backpack off the plane. I got it on the next plane and the flight was perfect. We make it to Anchorage and are waiting at the conveyor belt for the luggage and my backpack was the very first thing to come out.

"I'd wondered how a bird was going to make it in the luggage compartment, so on the way out I took a pigeon in the backpack, and it survived fine so I figured the gyrfalcon would make it. When I looked in my backpack at the airport, the bird went, *Gack gack gack gack,* so I ran over to the postal service parking lot and, thank God, there's my bus with a box in it all ready for the gyrfalcon."

They drove straight out of Alaska. When they reached Canadian customs, it was raining hard and the border inspector turned out to be a young woman who came out with an umbrella and asked them to come inside. Steve's friend started flirting with her, and the next thing they knew, they were in Canada on the AlCan Highway. Along the way, they stopped and shot birds to feed the gyrfalcon. They studied a map and headed for the smallest border crossing, which happened to be in Montana. It turned out to be a tiny building on a tiny road. Before reaching the border, they stopped and cleaned the bus to eliminate all signs of birds. The VW bus had built-in cupboards along one side, so Steve designed a false compartment in one of the cupboards to hold the gyrfalcon. Then he packed the cupboards so full of filthy clothes, if someone opened the door, he or she would gag. As it happened, the border guard stopped the bus, looked around, and waved them through.

"So," said Steve. "We got through customs and I got out BBG—short for Baby Bird Gyr—and lit up a great big cigar and drove into the United States with my bird sitting on my lap."

9

Legal Troubles

STEVE'S BEEN COMING to this little corner of Wyoming since 1987, when he got banned from hunting in the state of Utah for a year. "That's it," he'd said. "I'm never going to hunt in the state of Utah again." Except for the sky trials, and maybe a couple of other times.

In the mid-1980s, Steve and another falconer, Jim Hatchett, had gotten nailed for hunting with a peregrine out of season. Steve had been training a young female peregrine named Nakita in the weeks leading up to the hunting season. To do this, he took his bird out into an agricultural field not far from his home in Centerville, and Jim came along and ran his dogs at the same time so the bird could get used to dogs being under it.

When a falconer trains a young bird, he takes it out to the field to get it used to flying and to build up its endurance. He also wants to get a peregrine to fly high in the sky and wait on, or make circles in the sky over the falconer. When the bird is high enough, the falconer will often release a farm-raised game bird, such as a pheasant or a duck (called bagged game), or will throw some homing pigeons for the young falcon to chase. The point is to get the falcon to associate the falconer with food. Under the best circumstances, the falconer wants to have the bird catch the released game bird so that it feels successful. When the falconer decides the bird has had enough exercise or training for the day, he calls the bird back by blowing on a whistle and swinging a lure, a leather pouch that often has meat or the wing of a game bird attached to it. The bird will hear the whistle and see the lure and will stoop, or dive, down to the leather pouch. This is what happens in a perfect world.

In reality, the falconer has very little control over what happens when a young bird first leaves the fist. It can fly up and sit on a telephone pole. It can start chasing birds that are flying by, leaving the falconer on the ground saying, "Oh, shit!" as his bird soars out of sight. It might fly high, it might fly low. It might chase the bagged game bird. It might not. The falconer has no control over the mind of the bird; the bird may decide to catch a thermal and rise up out of sight and take off for new adventures. Over the years, falconers have discovered that what little control they have lies in the falcons' viewing them as the source of food and, later, as equal hunting partners. For this reason, birds of prey are flown when they're hungry so that they'll be motivated to fly hard and catch some dinner.

Two days before the duck-hunting season opened, when Steve and Jim were out in the field training Steve's bird, she flew off over a little hill and disappeared. Steve took off running after her. When he popped over the little hill he saw a man standing near what he recognized as Nakita sitting on a dead duck. The man had been driving slowly by, scouting the fields for geese and ducks in preparation for hunting season, when he saw what he'd thought was a goose flopping around in a field. He'd gotten out of his car and walked toward it to investigate. Steve called out to the man that it was his bird and to not touch her. The man was pretty excited by what he was watching and stood and talked to Steve as Steve tried to get his bird off the duck. When the bird wouldn't let go, Steve tore the wing off the duck and held it in his gloved hand, and the falcon got up on his glove to feed. In a minute or two Steve substituted part of a quail he had in his game bag for the duck wing and threw the wing down near the duck's body. In the meantime, another man approached them and identified himself as a game warden. He proceeded to give Steve and Jim (as an accomplice) tickets for the unlawful taking of protected wildlife and for training dogs on wild game birds out of season.

This was a terrible blow to Steve. He had trained his bird in that field about fifteen times prior to his bird nailing the duck—in fact, he had been training and flying birds in that field since 1973. The ducks and geese had just come in a couple of days earlier, and before he'd put his bird up that day, he had walked through the field and flushed all the geese and ducks from the area. They had flown out of his sight, so when he unhooded Nakita, he couldn't imagine there was any chance his bird would get distracted by a duck, much less catch one. It was almost unheard-of for a bird as young as his—only about four or five months old—to go after a big mallard duck that was twice its size and weight.

Ironically, if he had not ripped the wing off the duck after it had been killed by the falcon, he probably would have gotten off under the "let it lay" law, which recognizes that occasionally a game bird will be killed out of season by a trained falcon, but in that case, the falconer is not to touch the dead bird and must leave it where the falcon dropped it. But Steve hadn't wanted to force his bird off the kill, because he was afraid the bird would then associate Steve with taking away its food when it killed something rather than rewarding it. So in Steve's mind, the only responsible thing he could have done was what he did. He wasn't about to ruin his bird over this dead duck, and it wasn't as though he'd been planning to take the wing with him. Plus, he thought, the duck couldn't get any deader, so what was the problem?

The farmer who owned the field had seen Steve and Jim training the bird two nights before and had noticed a huge flock of geese and some ducks taking off from the newly cut oat field where they had been feeding. The next night he'd seen the men again, as did his son-in-law, who thought he saw the falcon chasing a duck. He'd called the Utah Fish and Game department because he didn't know if the falcon should be out there with all the game birds. Randy Peck was the game warden who'd been assigned to check out what was going on, and he must have thought he had died and gone to heaven when he saw who the falconer was.

Several years earlier, Randy Peck had gone undercover in a Fish and Game sting operation set up to nail falconers flying illegal birds. Peck posed as a falconer from Washington who was new to the area and wanted to meet some of the local falconers.

"This guy came to my house in a Jeep with a goshawk in it. He had a beard and said his name was Randy Robinson," said Steve. "He'd show up periodically over the next couple of years. He never got anything off me in that investigation."

In the meantime, a friend of Steve's brother who worked for Fish and Game told Steve that Robinson was actually an undercover agent, so Steve eventually confronted him.

"Robinson said, 'How can you say that? I'm your friend.' I told him if he was who he said he was then to just give me two names of falconers in Washington so I can verify that. Give them to me right now or just get out of here and don't ever come back."

According to Steve, the whole thing snowballed. Peck went back to his office and said his cover was blown, then another falconer told Peck who had ratted him out, and that guy got fired. The guy who got fired then produced evidence that the Fish and Game chief of law enforcement had misused public funds, using the state's money to do things like get a houseboat on Lake Powell and go on trips to see friends. There was a big exposé in the paper, and the chief got fired.

"Randy looked really bad to everyone because he hadn't gotten a single arrest and the whole department got shook down," said Steve. "Peck really hated me and wanted to get me."

So Randy Peck was right there when Steve's bird got that duck in the field. Then, it was just Steve's luck that Randy Peck's brother-in-law was the prosecuting attorney for the state. "And you know they had been talking about me for years. I was like Jesse James to them," said Steve. "I'm not kidding."

Steve was so pissed off after being ticketed in the field that he decided to take the case to trial; it turned out to be the most expensive misdemeanor trial ever held in the state of Utah. There was some hoopla in the paper at the time because his misdemeanor trial cost the state more than a concurrent murder trial in which a father had killed his son. Steve spent fifteen thousand dollars on his lawyer, who called nine people to the stand, including Steve. The prosecution called seven. The trial took several days.

The 561-page trial transcript is in two volumes and is a little window into what happens when falconers come up against normal people. The falconers tend to lose because they just sound too intense and rarefied, and eventually people wonder why the hell these guys are doing such a crazy sport anyway. During the trial, the jurors learned that peregrines were an endangered species; they learned how to hunt with birds; how to train young peregrines; how peregrines fly; how mallard ducks fly; and how big a mallard is compared with a peregrine. They heard that falconers don't own their birds, that the birds are owned by the federal government. They heard terms like *jesses, leashes, lures,* and *waiting on, ringing up,* and *tail chase.* They heard Steve characterized as both callously indifferent to wildlife and passionately devoted to birds. They heard he was the mountain region director for the North American Falconers' Association (NAFA). They found out he did the popular bird show at the Tracy Aviary in Salt Lake, where he'd trained birds to fly over the heads of the audience. They also learned that he served pigeons to his falcon as a way to train it to catch prey. They saw diagrams of fields complete with sight lines. They heard about the Fish and Game stakeout where game wardens had sat with scopes and binoculars trained on the field. They listened to stories of falcons being electrocuted by power poles and ducks being bounced out of the sky by birds of prey. Utah's a hunting state, but this may have been too much even for them.

Steve's lawyer did a good job but didn't really talk about the "let it lay" law, which might have made a difference in the case. Something about Steve pulling the wing off that duck probably stuck with the jurors. There was also some conflicting testimony: the farmer's son-in-law said he'd seen a falcon or a hawk chasing a duck the day before Steve got nailed, whereas Steve said the falcon had been chasing a pigeon. It also didn't help that the state's witnesses were farmers and relatives of farmers and game wardens, and the witnesses for the defense were high-powered, intense falconers and raptor researchers and biologists. And, finally, the state got the last word and characterized Steve as acting "knowingly and recklessly with regard to the safety of the duck."

"Remember," said the prosecutor. "What we're talking about is not regulating falcons; we're talking about protecting the wild life. Protecting the duck, and those ducks were not protected the way they ought to have been protected." He continued.

Now, why are we talking about this? Why is it so important that we're talking about this duck? Look at the organization that you've got here, the people that you've had testify . . . Who testified here in behalf of the defense? You look at the list, the exhibits that the defendants put forward that talks about the statistics for falconry, and it will tell you that there are only about fifty falconers in the whole state that do this as a sport to take birds. And you've heard from fully ten percent of those people. They're a tight-knit group—they've got this club that has got presidents and secretaries and does correspondence and publishes a newsletter and has meets and trials and parties, and all these different activities, they're a close-knit group and they're there to protect their interests so that they can participate in this activity unbridled.

And that's what the meaning of this case is, because to those people, we're talking about what they can do when they go out. Are we going to enforce this law or are we not going to enforce this law?

The defendants were out there testing the law. What are we going to do if the Fish and Game comes and checks us out, oh, we just say it's an incidental kill because we threw a pigeon up; but the officer had his eyes trained on them the whole time and that pigeon was never there. And those two falconers knew that this falcon would pursue a duck.

Now, they can say that it wouldn't—that they didn't think it would kill the duck—but they knew at least it would pursue it, because it had been pursuing it on the days before; at least there was a strong likelihood, and that's all that's required for a taking. Remember, part of the definition of taking is to pursue.

We call it illegal taking, but it's really designed to protect the birds from hunters who are out there before they shoot—we don't have to wait until they shoot, or put their falcon up before we can arrest them or cite them for violating this law. But in this case, the unmistakable issue—the unmistakable fact—is that a duck died.

And we can parade all the experts you want up here to this stand to say I don't think that falcon could have taken the duck, I don't think that falcon could have done this; but the fact is, it did. It killed the duck.

Steve didn't really stand a chance. He and Jim got off on the dog-training charge but were fined—Steve was fined $1,000 and got 180 days in jail, which was suspended, and Jim was fined $750 and got the same suspended jail sentence—and they had their hunting licenses revoked for a year for the unlawful taking of protected wildlife. That rankles Steve to this day, and he wondered why the lawyer didn't go after the ownership issue. In his mind, since the government owned the bird he was flying, then how could he be punished for what the government's bird did? And as I heard this, I thought that an esoteric argument like that was not the way to win the hearts and minds of a local jury.

Under the federal laws governing falconry, a falconer's bird is owned by the feds. It doesn't matter if the bird was taken from the wild or produced in a breeder's chamber. The laws were written before falcons could be produced by captive breeding, and they were written to protect the birds, not the falconers. So every falconer struggles with the ownership issue because the federal authorities can confiscate the birds at any time—birds that the falconer raised, trained, and loved.

The case was appealed to the state supreme court, and it lost on the same principle: a falconer is responsible for his bird when it makes a kill, even if the bird has gotten lost. "In my mind, that proves ownership," said Steve. "Means that someone can find a falcon that's been gone for ten years on a duck and that falconer is still responsible because he still owns that bird. Right now the government can have it both ways and say they own our birds for licensing and then not own them when the bird is lost."

After Steve's conviction, he tried not to hunt sage grouse in Utah—didn't want to hunt sage grouse in Utah because he hated Fish and Game—but ultimately, he couldn't withstand the temptation. But he gave in to the temptation for a good cause—it was all about hunting with Jomo, his male (also called a tiercel) gyrfalcon-peregrine hybrid.

It turned out Steve was still on Fish and Game's radar screen. His friend the noted bird trainer and falconer Steve

Martin came to Utah to visit Steve and wanted to hunt with his bird Millie in Park Valley, a gorgeous area about a hundred and fifty miles north of Salt Lake. Steve and Steve Martin loaded up their birds and dogs and headed out for a nice flying field that had sage grouse in it. It was Jomo's first flying season, and Steve had him in the back of the truck along with a bagged pheasant. Although Steve's hunting license in Utah had been suspended, as a falconer he was still able to train his birds, meaning it was okay to have Jomo fly on bagged game.

Park Valley is a drive of several hours from Steve's home in Centerville. They got to the field, and Steve Martin's bird Millie had several flights on sage grouse but didn't catch anything, so the falconers sat by their truck and had lunch. Then Steve decided to fly Jomo. He got him out of the truck and put him up, waiting for him to get higher before he released the pheasant into the field. As Jomo was ringing up, a crippled grouse broke out of some cover near the truck and began to fly away. Steve had that *oh, shit!* moment as he watched the grouse and then watched Jomo, but Jomo didn't stoop on the bird. Steve couldn't figure out why his young falcon hadn't chased the grouse, and he began to fret that the interruption in hunting, thanks to his suspended license, had ruined his bird.

Steve released the bagged pheasant as Jomo got into position overhead, and the falcon nailed the game bird as it began to fly away. Just then a man came walking toward Steve Martin and asked to see his hunting license. It was a game warden. The two falconers showed their federal falconry permits, Steve showed his Wyoming hunting license, and Steve Martin showed his hunting licenses, including his temporary license to hunt game in Utah. As the game warden looked at the licenses, Steve explained that he was training his falcon and not hunting and that the pheasant the falcon was currently sitting on had been a bagged pheasant. When Steve said he had to go get his bird, the warden left.

Apparently, the next day the warden went into his office and said he'd seen some falconers hunting in Park Valley. When he mentioned who they were, one of the Fish and Game wardens recognized Steve Chindgren's name. Several days later, Steve was at the Tracy Aviary getting ready for a bird show when game wardens showed up, blocked all the entrances and exits with their trucks, and approached Steve. And in front of his employees, they said, "Steve Chindgren? You're under arrest for hunting without a license," and proceeded to handcuff him, read him his rights, and lead him away. All Steve could think as he was taken to one of the Fish and Game trucks was *How am I going to go home and tell my wife we're going to trial again?* He said it felt like someone was ripping his heart out. In addition, even though Steve said he wasn't guilty, the aviary fired him right away because they couldn't afford to be on the wrong side of Fish and Game.

Steve opted for another jury trial, only this time he hired a good criminal lawyer and was acquitted.

"Fish and Game was all excited because here I was on probation, and if they got a conviction I was going to jail. They were sure they were going to win and that I was going to serve time," said Steve. "But we won that case. There were some falconers in the back of the room who whooped and hollered just like in a movie when the jury came out and said not guilty. It was a real relief to walk out of the courtroom a free man."

About a year later, Steve was hunting in Park Valley again, this time with Robert Bagley, owner of Marshall Telemetry, and some visitors from England. They had a bird up and were running some dogs, and all of a sudden a biologist who worked for the state came up to them, screaming, "I can't believe what I'm seeing, I can't believe what I'm seeing." Steve didn't know what the man was talking about and asked, "What are you seeing?" The biologist replied, "I see falconers running a dog from the vehicle. I thought falconry was an honorable sport, and that's the laziest thing I've ever seen." Steve listened to him go on and on and finally said he had a bird up and the dogs were on point, and he told the biologist that he should watch what promised to be a beautiful flight. "I refuse to watch," he said, and Steve said he didn't care what he did and went and flushed a grouse, which Jomo chased down. Bagley was horrified and said later that the Europeans just couldn't believe how they'd been treated in the field.

The biologist, who was also a gun hunter and liked to hunt grouse, tried to convince Fish and Game that the falconry season was too long. They wouldn't close the season, but the biologist did persuade them to close automobile access to several areas, including the one Steve was hunting, after the gun hunting season ended. The gun hunting season on grouse lasts for three days in October, whereas the falconry season lasts for months. That meant that if Steve wanted to hunt in those fields, he'd have to hike in there with his dog on a lead while carrying his bird and all his telemetry equipment. "They said it's a sensitive wildlife area in the winter," said Steve. "But I knew it was just to keep me from hunting there."

Soon after that, the state started making noises about the sage grouse being an endangered species in Utah and decided that the falconers—like the gun hunters—would be able to take only two grouse during the entire season and would have to apply for tags to be able to hunt them. "You couldn't take only two grouse over a few months and be a successful falconer," said Steve. Apparently Fish and Game thought falconers were catching a lot of grouse. Since Steve had decided to fly his birds almost exclusively on sage grouse by that point, this was the nail in the Utah coffin for him. Steve says that since that law was put into place in the past five years only three grouse have been taken by falconers in the state of Utah, although he says there are a lot of grouse out there. The falconers just aren't flying on sage grouse in Utah anymore.

10

Operation Falcon

SEVERAL YEARS AGO, Tim, the kids, and I drove to down-
state New York to attend a bird of prey day that's held annually
at Green Chimneys, a school for kids with emotional, behav-
ioral, and learning problems. Green Chimneys has been around
for about sixty years and is a worldwide leader in animal-
assisted therapy. I wanted to go because I wanted to see all the
neat birds, but I also wanted to see Robert Kennedy Jr., a local falconer and a son of Bobby Kennedy, who was going to be
speaking at the event. While we were there, a man Tim had
recently met at a New York State Falconry Association meet
called him over to look in the back of his truck. "Look at these,"
he said, as he raised a towel that was covering a dishpan sitting
on the truck bed. Under the towel were three gyrfalcon chicks
that were only several days old. They were at the stage between
gangly dinosaur-like newborn and downy puffball. They looked
up at him expectantly with their beaks open in a kind of silent
plea. Soon they'd be for sale.

There's nothing quite so spectacular-looking as a big white
female gyrfalcon—the sheer size of the bird as she stands over
two feet tall from her tail to the top of her head is impressive.
And when she opens her wings and they span four feet, you can
almost see and feel the Arctic in her; you can imagine her flying
low over scrubby tundra in search of ptarmigan and then com-

ing to rest on orange lichen–covered rocks. There's a promise of speed and power in her bearing. You look at her and know that whatever you chose to fly her on would be toast.

And then there's the peregrine. This has always been the bird to fly for those who are really serious about flying falcons. Peregrines are fast and fierce and drop like bullets from the sky in spectacular flights on game. They are deadly. Historically, they were flown by European royalty. Who wouldn't want a bird like this? Before the peregrine population crashed as a result of eggshell thinning caused by residual effects of DDT, and before government regulation of these birds, falconers would go to places like Assateague Island off the Atlantic Coast and Padre Island off the Texas coast in the Gulf of Mexico to trap peregrines who were on their two-thousand-mile migration from the Arctic to South America. In the early days of trapping at Assateague or Padre, a falconer would have a friend bury him on the beach so that only his head was above the sand, and then the friend would camouflage the falconer's head with beach grass. In one buried hand the falconer held a line tied to a pigeon. When an exhausted, hungry peregrine swooped down on what looked like fast food, the falconer would emerge from the sand like a sand worm in a *Star Wars* movie and grab the peregrine.

Many of the falconers I've met are covetous of birds. This doesn't mean a falconer will do anything to get a bird he wants, but if an opportunity presents itself, he'll have a very hard time saying no. Coveting these birds can be like a fire that burns in a falconer's brain. Maybe he can't think of anything else and imagines that if he only had that bird, he'd have the prettiest, fastest, most deadly bird in the field. That thought consumes him, and if he has to go outside the law, or maybe just interpret the law loosely, then, well, maybe he'll do it because he can justify it in his head. He tells himself the law is flawed. Then it takes no time at all before the falconer believes that because he wants the bird, it should be his. He tells himself he'll love it and take care of it and turn it into the best hunting hawk ever.

Both the federal government and the official organization of falconers, the North American Falconers' Association, seem to recognize this trait, because they've made licensing and the laws governing falconry stringent. Until 1972, there were no laws governing falconry. In fact, in many parts of the country fish and game departments paid a bounty on every hawk, falcon, and owl shot because those raptors were regarded as varmints who had a taste for farm animals. There's a famous 1930s photograph taken by Richard Pough in which he lined up hundreds of dead raptors he'd found on Hawk Mountain, a popular place to shoot birds out of the sky as they cruised past during fall migration. This photo led to the creation of Hawk Mountain Bird Sanctuary, which today attracts scores of birders who hike up onto the ridge during the peak spring and fall raptor migration and stand armed with binoculars and scopes where shotgun-wielding people once stood shoulder to shoulder. Pough went on to become the first president of the Nature Conservancy.

The federal falconry law establishes three levels of falconer—apprentice, general, and master. The process of rising through the ranks takes years. If you're interested in becoming a falconer, first you have to take a written exam. If you pass, you can be an apprentice falconer, and then you have to find a sponsor—a general or master falconer willing to oversee and sign off on your training. Along the way there are checks and balances and hoops to be jumped through, ensuring—the government hopes—that a wannabe falconer will receive guidance and training. The law codifies what birds can be flown at which level and how many birds the falconer is allowed to fly. (At this point, that number is three, but falconers like Steve would love to see the limit raised to five.) It also stipulates that an apprentice falconer must wild-trap his first falconry bird—generally a red-tailed hawk or a kestrel, depending on the state. This is supposed to weed out the fascinated dabblers. The presumption is that a red-tail is hardy, and if things don't go so well, it can pretty easily be released back into the wild. An apprentice soon learns how hard it is to build a mews and to trap and care for birds at the same time as he or she is learning how to be a falconer. Only those with a burning passion for the sport make it through the first year. As the falconer ascends the pecking order in American falconry, he's allowed to take from the nest or wild-trap all sorts of raptors. The type of bird that's allowed to be taken and flown depends on the laws of each state. At this point, in a few western states there are some provisions for taking young peregrines from the nest. This totally galls some birding groups, such as Audubon, who point out that it wasn't so long ago that peregrines were on the endangered species list. Peregrines were only removed from the federal list in 1999, and they then became the poster birds for bird-recovery programs. Longwingers like Tim and Steve are waiting for the day when they can legally go to a place such as Padre and trap a wild tundrius peregrine as it migrates through.

Federal law also regulates propagators, or breeders, of raptors. Falcon breeders must be licensed falconers and are allowed to give or sell birds only to other licensed falconers.

The federal falconry law seems almost as arcane as the sport of falconry. It stipulates in part that the birds used for falconry—whether wild-trapped or captive-bred or hybrid birds raised in a chamber—belong to the government and that the falconer is acting as a caretaker of the bird. In a way, this makes sense: the primary objective of the law is to protect the birds, and under the law all raptors are protected as migratory birds. But it's also bizarre, because it places a hybrid bird that is the result of years of selective crossbreeding between species in the same category as a wild-trapped bird, and while the wild raptor can exist in nature, the hybrid cannot.

This system is propped up by a whole lot of paperwork,

which can lead to a strained relationship between the natural resources officials who enforce the falconry laws and the falconers. So falconers live under constant threat—real or perceived—that their birds can be confiscated by the feds at any time. And for many of the falconers I know, this does not sit well.

Many falconers, particularly those older than about forty, consider the early 1980s a low point in North American falconry. That's when officials in Canada and the United States set up a sting operation—known as Operation Falcon—to catch falconers in the act of illegally selling much sought after gyrfalcons to the Arabs. The belief was that these North American birds were being sold for as much as $100,000 each, breaking several laws under the Migratory Bird Treaty Act and CITES. The U.S. Fish and Wildlife Service enlisted the aid of Jeff McPartlin, a falconer in Montana, to help them entrap falconers in the United States. According to *The Pilgrim and the Cowboy*, by Paul McKay, the only book written about the subject, McPartlin had a bone to pick with many of America's preeminent falconers because he felt he had been snubbed by them over the years, so he jumped at the chance to get even.

McPartlin's modus operandi was to contact a falconer and say he had a beautiful gyrfalcon for sale. In the early 1980s, the only way to acquire a gyrfalcon was to trap one legally somewhere in one of the western states. The problem with this was that very few gyrfalcons strayed south of the border, preferring the cool Arctic north. It was illegal to trap a gyrfalcon in Alaska or Canada and then transport it across the border. A couple of falconers had gyrfalcons, and many who had seen them fly wanted these magnificent birds for their own, so McPartlin's offer was irresistible to some falconers. The gyrfalcons McPartlin was passing on had been trapped in Canada by U.S. Fish and Wildlife officials and given to him to use as bait. The catch was that these gyrfalcons wouldn't have the proper paperwork or any leg bands—all legal falcons had to have leg bands that identified them.

Operation Falcon would have been funny if it weren't so pathetic. Here was the federal government trying to uncover a big smuggling operation that they soon found out didn't exist, and in the meantime they took birds from the wild and tried their hardest to ensnare falconers in a scheme. By appealing to the covetous nature of falconers, they enticed some of them to do things they shouldn't have done. In the end, there were sixty-eight convictions for breaking U.S. federal wildlife laws (five were felony convictions and the rest were misdemeanors), bringing in $500,000 in fines. Compare these fines with the Operation Falcon five-year investigation and prosecution budget, which, according to McKay, certainly exceeded $2 million. The thirty-six gyrfalcons the U.S. Fish and Wildlife Service took from the wild and sold, traded, or gave away were worth—at a modest retail value of $20,000 each—a sum of $720,000.

What the government failed to find was an organized ring of falcon smugglers supplying gyrfalcons to the Arabs for big wads of cash. Instead, the federal government found out that falconers were very vulnerable to that kind of appeal and would sometimes go outside the law to obtain beautiful birds to fly. My husband, Tim, compared it to being presented with an opportunity to spend the night with Marilyn Monroe and said, "Who could resist?" People are vulnerable in lots of ways. Few of the misdemeanor convictions involved schemes for commercial profit; most involved falconers who had bought or traded illegal birds for personal use only. Almost all of the convictions involved deals falconers made with McPartlin, who regularly sold falcons at cut-rate prices, traded for them, or simply gave them away.

More than twenty years after Operation Falcon went down, there are still falconers who will not talk about what happened during that investigation and who get very close-mouthed if you bring it up because they see the whole episode as nothing more than persecution of falconers by the federal government.

Steve came within a hairsbreadth of being entrapped by Mc-Partlin. McPartlin sent someone to Steve's house who said, "Jeff McPartlin heard you flew gyrfalcons and he knows you don't have one at the moment. He wants you to give him a call because he has a legal bird for you." Steve knew there was something fishy about this, so he told the guy he didn't think he'd do it. The falconer came back a while later and said, "McPartlin still has that bird and he'd really like you to have it and all you have to do is call him." Steve kept imagining having another gyrfalcon, so he thought about it long and hard. In a way, Steve was particularly vulnerable to this offer because he had already flown gyrfalcons and knew how great they were. He really, really wanted another one. So he picked up the phone and dialed the number the falconer had given him. It was busy, and Steve never called back. Later he realized just how lucky he had been.

11

Steve's Falcons

LIKE MOST FALCONERS, Steve tries to keep copious notes in his falconry journals about his birds. During the hunting season, it can be almost impossible to catch more than a few minutes to write anything, so at the very least he records what the falcons weigh on any particular day, where they went hunting, and what they killed. At the end of each season, he tallies the number of head of game each bird has taken.

The very first entry in his leather-bound falconry journal of 1988–1990 says "Jomo is a gyr/peregrine tiercel made from silver gyr semen obtained from Vic Hardiswick, S.D. AI into a female 1/4 peales, 3/8 brookii, and 3/8 shaheen made by Lester Boyd, W.A. Jomo was hatched at my facilities and is the first gyr/peregrine I have produced." Jomo is a made bird—not in the Mafia sense, but in the sense that he is the product of a union that could never have occurred in nature. The gyrfalcon semen from South Dakota artificially inseminated a bird of varying races of peregrine—Peale's, a Spanish race, and a race of falcon from the Middle East—which came from a breeder in Washington. Jomo was hatched and raised in Steve's mews in his backyard in Centerville, Utah.

The journal entries about Jomo show that at first this bird was very difficult. He would leave Steve's fist and chase doves out of sight. He had a hard time getting the idea of waiting on or paying attention to the falconer down below—the hunting partner who would provide game. Steve flew him almost exclusively on sage grouse right from the beginning. In Jomo's first season he took eleven grouse, although most of them, Steve wrote, had something wrong with them and one, taken in Rich County, Utah, was wearing a radio transmitter.

During that first season, Steve used more than one hundred game-farm pheasants to train Jomo. The bird got easily discouraged hunting grouse, so Steve would flush the grouse off the point and throw a pheasant up with them. This worked well to build Jomo's confidence because he could always catch the pheasant. By the beginning of his second season, he had molted into a beautiful silver bird looking very much like a small jerkin, or male gyrfalcon.

For Jomo's second season, Steve bought a two-hundred-fifty-dollar sage grouse hunting permit for the Deseret Land and Livestock Ranch in Utah. He felt that the months of September and October of Jomo's second season were critical for his training because the sage grouse were still in brood groups of hens and almost full-grown young; they were plentiful and would be a little easier to catch than they would be later. Steve's favorite hunting area at Deseret was a field called Twelve Towers, named for the sprinkler system. "Jomo became a grouse hawk in this field," Steve wrote.

"The single most important factor in making a good grouse hawk is to have a good grouse dog. From my observations the English pointer is the best choice of dog. They are stupid but have a strong desire to hunt and are incredibly tough with tremendous endurance." When Steve wrote these words he had a black-and-white English pointer named Pete that he ran out of the truck to locate grouse. Pete occasionally pointed rabbits, but, like the dogs Steve has today, Pete would leave the rabbits alone if Steve yelled, "Find birds." Steve discovered that it was easy to tell the difference between a rabbit point and a grouse point. If he smelled a rabbit, Pete would stop suddenly to look at a bush. With grouse, the dog would begin to line up for about two hundred yards, depending on the breeze, and then work in toward the birds, moving slower and slower as he neared the grouse and ending with a solid point. Steve also observed that Pete's tail was usually curled when he was pointing a rabbit and straight when pointing grouse.

Jomo was successful hunting the young grouse on the Deseret Ranch. Because Steve always ran a dog in the field when he flew Jomo, the falcon soon learned that a dog on point meant birds. As Jomo's second season progressed, Steve began hunting in the sagebrush deserts around Farson, Wyoming. While in Wyoming, Jomo began to take higher and higher pitches—or flew higher into the sky—and Steve found that once the bird learned to identify when a dog was on point, he began to fly better.

Jomo learned the secret to being the most successful grouse hawk I've ever seen. The secret is taught by the falconer. Once a falcon has knocked down a grouse and is pitching up into the wind, send the other dog in immediately to reflush the grouse allowing the falcon to rake over and either strike the grouse or bind in the air. Sage grouse will stay on the ground and lure the falcon down only to fly leaving the falcon in the sagebrush! Once a falcon learns to stay on the wing and work with you and the dogs, the grouse are in big trouble. The only grouse that will escape are the ones that do not get knocked to the ground. Jomo weighs 26 oz so it is imperative that he have a vertical stoop. Most of the time this works out but every now and then something goes wrong with the flush. Jomo learned that if a grouse is at all out of position his only chance is to bind, releasing the grouse just before impact with the ground, leaving him to command the air. Depending on the conditions and circumstances, I will either flush as he pitches up or let him remount and then flush. It was in his second season he saw his first sharp-tailed grouse, which he took easily, and also his first prairie chicken was taken. Because Jomo has learned to stay in the air, the grouse have little chance if they stay on the ground after the first strike. The dogs will check if the grouse can fly and it will be knocked down again and it is curtains for them.

Jomo took an astounding 105 grouse his second season.

Over the past twenty years Steve has flown as many birds at any one time as is permitted by law. He has a propagation permit, and this means he can fly three birds on his federal falconry permit while he trains two birds on his propagation permit to get them ready for sale. There seems to be a gray area in the law about training a bird and hunting with a bird, and this is the same pit Steve fell into when he was charged with illegally taking wildlife while he was training his bird in Utah. Because Steve knows this can be dicey, he's established a good relationship and rapport with many of the Game and Fish people in Wyoming. During one cold, cold January when I was in Wyoming watching Steve hunt, he had a little meltdown every day because another falconer had come to stay for a while but hadn't bothered to get a Wyoming hunting permit.

"You can't do this," said Steve. "You have to go to Green River and get a permit before you hunt with me in any of my spots because if you get caught, that will put me on the radar screen." He was livid for much of the time, and that guest, an honest to God falconry bum who spent about six months on the road with his falcons and his dog following game to hunt, didn't really care. He didn't even pretend to care. As far as I know, he never did get a permit. Neither of his birds caught a grouse, either, but not for a lack of trying.

Because Steve flies so many birds, there's a hell of a lot of flying every day during the hunting season for sage grouse, which in Wyoming stretches from September 1 through February. And he's consistent about the flying order. Jomo always gets the first flight, then Steve cycles through the birds, from oldest to youngest. Jahanna, whom Steve began to regard as Jomo's replacement, went second. If there is someone who's also flying birds with Steve, that person may get the third flight if he's lucky. Most people are just happy to be out in the field with Steve watching him fly his birds, and they'll take a flight whenever he gives it to them.

This is Jomo's twentieth season and he's definitely slowing down. Steve's going to try to have another good season with him but is also planning something a little different. Instead of just flying him on sage grouse, he's planning to fly him on each of the game birds in the area. He'll fly Jomo in five states—Nebraska, Idaho, Kansas, Montana, and Wyoming—on lesser and greater prairie chickens, sharp-tailed grouse, pheasant, sage grouse, and duck. "We'll see if he can do it," Steve said. "I think he can catch them all—he's kind of losing it but he still flies okay. Probably the greater prairie chickens will be the hardest, but Jomo's so smart, he'll figure out how to do it." Steve thinks taking Jomo on this kind of quest is the appropriate way for the bird to end his career.

Jomo was eighteen when Steve started seeing signs of aging in him. He was clearly slowing down and not interested in going after the big cock birds anymore. He even looked older as he sat on his perch—kind of stooped over, with less than perfect-looking feathers and a missing talon. Steve told me he'd seen a gyrfalcon sitting like that at an eyrie in Alaska and had thought to himself, *That's an old hag* (*haggard* is a falconry term for a wild bird older than a year). Steve said that he accepted that Jomo was an old bird and that his time could come any day. "It's almost sadder seeing him not perform because he was so dynamic," he said. "It'd almost be better if something happens to him while he's hunting rather than see him . . . but he's a good bird." People have suggested that Steve retire Jomo and not fly him anymore, but Steve is resistant to this idea. "This is the only life he's ever known," he said. "He knows what's expected of him, and he'll keep trying, and I think it'll keep him in better health." But he sees the toll that flying sage grouse all these years has taken on the bird. Steve makes the comparison that every single time Jomo catches a big cock bird it's like going a few rounds with Mike Tyson because the grouse are so much bigger than his falcon. It's no wonder that today, Jomo—who's probably arthritic and sore every time he flies—takes one look at what's flushed and won't go after the big ones anymore.

But none of this stops Steve from taking Jomo out day after day and putting him up in all kinds of weather. It can be a blazing-hot morning or one that's bitter cold. Or a quiet, still morning or one with a stiff desert breeze that makes the woody sagebrush rustle as the prickly branches brush against one another. Or a lovely autumn day or maybe one in deep winter with the snow blowing sideways across the two-track. And Jomo takes it all in and then heads toward the sky, a little slower, perhaps, than a decade ago. And as Jomo's sore arthritic wings pump hard to gain altitude, Steve looks at him and a flicker of recognition crosses his face.

He feels the aches and pains in himself as the bird rings up above the dog on point. And he knows he's caught in a bind. For twenty years, his job as the falconer has been to provide Jomo the best hunting opportunity available. But since Jomo won't hit the big birds anymore and Steve can't be sure of scaring up a smaller hen bird, each flight might very well end as so many others have recently, with Jomo being called down to the lure after ignoring or delivering just a glancing blow to a cock bird that's burst from the thicket in front of a pointing dog. And the little disappointment Steve feels and is sure the bird feels every time this happens gets put away like pennies in a jar. And he knows that someday that jar will fill up.

When I was visiting Steve at his home in Centerville, he showed me a picture of Jomo with his daughter Jenna. Jomo was a young bird, and Jenna, who's now a beautiful young woman in her twenties, was just a toddler. She's always known Jomo. Julie, Steve's wife, doesn't have anything to do with the birds, but even she calls Jomo "the sweetest bird." Although Jomo's a full-on imprint, he bred naturally with a gyrfalcon for about five or six years. All in all, Jomo's "made" about twenty birds through either natural or artificial insemination. And he's been involved with raising a score more babies.

"Since I've had Jomo I don't know how many other falcons I've flown," said Steve. "They all get killed by eagles, and tons of eagles have tried to kill Jomo, but he's quick enough to get out of their way and smart enough to avoid them. He's so wary when he's out there. He's just a real smart bird."

Steve has had other birds that he's loved almost as much as Jomo. First there was BBG, the white gyrfalcon he took from a nest in Alaska and smuggled back over the border. Then there was Smokey, another white gyrfalcon. Both BBG and Smokey were electrocuted by power lines after they landed on electrical poles. When Steve found Smokey, the bird's eyes weren't even closed. He massaged the bird's chest and tried to give him mouth-to-mouth resuscitation in an effort to revive him.

Mouth-to-mouth seems like a weird move to do on a bird, but it wasn't the first time Steve had used a lifesaving maneuver on a falcon. Once he was with a falconer who was feeding up his bird in the field by giving him some grouse meat from a bird that Steve had gotten a couple of days earlier. After forty-eight hours or so, the grouse meat gets kind of sticky. Suddenly, some of the meat got stuck in the bird's trachea and it couldn't breathe. The falconer started screaming, *"My bird's dying! My bird's dying!"* and Steve saw that the bird wasn't getting any air at all. It was on the ground and going into convulsions, so he grabbed the bird and performed a Heimlich-like maneuver on it—*whomp whomp whomp*—forcing the air out of the bird and dislodging the meat. Steve saved the bird. He said it was the only thing he could think of doing—he wasn't going to sit there and watch it die without trying something. Most people wouldn't have thought to squeeze the air out of the bird, so without Steve, the bird would have died.

Before Jomo, the falcon Steve had owned the longest—and that was only half as long as Jomo—was Kallikak. She was one of the very first peregrine-prairie hybrids produced by breeders Steve Baptiste and Dave Jamieson. Steve had given them his first eyas prairie falcon. Kallikak was an imprint, and Steve said when he first started flying her she screamed so loudly that he wondered what he was going to do with her. It's hard to imagine how bad the screaming of a falcon can be if you've never heard it, but if you think of the sound a rusty hand pump might make—*errreeeeeee errreeeeeee errreeeeeee*—and then run that sound through an amplifier—*ERRREEEEEEE ERRREEEEEEE ERRREEEEEEE*—you'll come close. Steve knew he couldn't just release her because she was an imprint and hadn't been raised in the wild, but the first time he took her out, he flew her without telemetry. And of course she started chasing some birds and flew off into a marsh. "I didn't like the bird but I couldn't tell Baptiste and Jamieson that I lost her the first time I flew her," he said.

Duck season was opening the next weekend so he had five hundred fliers made up that said *Lost Falcon $100 Reward,* and he went to every access point in the marsh and posted the fliers. Then he rented a loudspeaker, put it on the top of his old gray Vega with the smashed-in side, drove out to the marsh on opening weekend, and announced that the person who had lost the falcon was in the gray Vega and if anyone found the bird to please contact the Vega for the reward. He got a call from a hunter who said he'd grabbed the bird when it landed on a duck he had shot. The hunter made Steve meet him at a grocery store first to show him the money, and after that, he took Steve to his bird, which was in a cage in the hunter's backyard.

Kallikak turned into the most successful duck hawk Steve ever had. She even hunted ducks that were on passage, or were flying high overhead, which is an unbelievable feat, especially for an imprint. One evening when Steve was in Brigham City with his bird, he stopped at a ditch that looked promising for ducks. He didn't use a dog in those days. People used to say that Steve was a pointer, a spaniel, and a Lab all in one because he was so dynamic when he ran and chased up quarry for his birds. So when Steve saw this ditch, he put Kallikak up and started running along it, hoping to scare up some ducks. The bird was way up when suddenly ducks flew beneath the falcon, and she stooped and knocked one down. Steve couldn't believe what he had just seen.

He took Kallikak to the same field night after night and watched the show through his binoculars. She'd get up really high and see the ducks coming into a neighboring cornfield from the marshes, so she'd lie in wait above them. She got so good at this that if she missed, she'd go right into a flock of ducks and stay with them, and although they'd ring up to try to get away from her, she'd go up with them and use them as cover and wait until another flock of ducks came beneath them. Then she'd break out and stoop at those ducks. "I had some great adventures with Kallikak," said Steve.

Kallikak was a screamer right from day one. Steve built a box for the top of his old gray Vega and transported her that way just so he wouldn't have to hear her scream. But she was also a brave bird. Once she hit a fence and broke her leg, and after it healed, when Steve first started flying her again, that leg would just dangle, so she'd strike or grab her quarry in the head with her good foot.

Like BBG, Smokey, and later Jomo, the one quarry that was really a challenge for Kallikak was sage grouse. In her eleventh season, she was killed while hunting sage grouse. She'd hit a grouse and then chased it into a draw, and by the time Steve got to her, a great horned owl had killed her. He had to walk two miles back to his car carrying his dead bird. When Steve talks about Kallikak and the adventures they had, it's with as much affection as when he talks about Jomo.

It's hard to imagine Steve without Jomo, his constant hunting partner for the past two decades, but that day will come soon, and on some level he knows it. As a way to hedge against what will likely be a crushing depression, Steve is starting to focus some of his attention on his four-year-old hybrid Jahanna. There are times when the younger bird is in the air that Steve will acknowledge how good he is—Jahanna is a high flyer and seems to have a real desire to hit the sage grouse as they fly as fast as they can across the desert floor. And at that point I see just a hint of a smile on Steve's face, as if he knows he's looking at the future—his future. This, he thinks, is the bird that will take him into old age.

12

The Cabin

IT'S A BRIGHT early-summer morning at the cabin. Cottontails hop around the sandy scrape of a backyard between the cabin and the pigeon coop in search of any tender green shoots that might have sprung up after last night's rain. Ground squirrels sit on their haunches nibbling things. Pigeons walk around the backyard, some of the male birds cooing *ooooo ooooo ooooo* as they persistently pursue females around and around the sandy yard in hopes that they'll get lucky. Dozens of pigeons spend the early part of the day teetering on a wire that goes from the main electric pole back toward the horse barn. Joe Harmer told me that they've found all manner of hawks and even a golden eagle dead—electrocuted—at the base of that pole, and they still can't get the electric company to make it raptor safe. Seems ironic that a falconer can't get a safe pole in his yard.

The desert starts right beyond the pigeon coop. When you're out there, you're walking on a matrix of really fine dust, and rocks—pebble-sized and larger. It feels flat and hard, and the ground sparkles as the sun catches the bits of mica and quartz in its rays. This time of year there are tufts of burned grass mixed in with the sagebrush, which is sometimes closely spaced and makes for prickly walking if your legs are bare. An eighteen-inch-high sagebrush can be a hundred years old. That's why people worry when they see concrete well pads for natural gas exploration and roads going in and then hear the oil and gas companies say they'll reclaim the land after scraping it clean. They wonder how people can replace a hundred-year-old sagebrush.

The gray-and-black-striped kitten heads away from the safety of the rear entryway and into the desert, stopping to look back every ten yards or so. I wonder if I'll see it again. A few days ago there were three kittens playing under a dug-away portion of the shed that holds the pigeon feed, and now there's just one. I'm sure someone dumped these kittens here, and it totally pisses me off. I've watched them and worried about them for days. I heard a faint mewing for hours the other day and walked toward the sound and found that the champagne-colored kitten had fallen down a pipe in the ground near the weathering yard. It was about six feet down. I rummaged around in the garage and came up with a nylon horse lead, and I figured out how to fasten one end at the top of the pipe using a variety of sticks and a heavy concrete weight I'd found (probably used to tether a hawk to), and then I dropped the other end into the pipe. The kitten hissed and spit. I had visions of that kitten climbing the rope to freedom and knew it wouldn't if it saw me, so I went inside. About an hour later it was still in the pipe and I saw that gray clouds were gathering into what looked like a big piece of dirty cotton batting in the sky. Then I heard the thunder and saw some lightning in the distance. I was frantic about the kitten. I took one of my long-sleeved shirts, tied knots in several places to make it skinnier, then tied it to the end of the horse lead and dropped it into the pipe, thinking it might be easier to climb out on the fabric. Again, hissing and spitting.

The winds began picking up, and I felt like Dorothy in *The Wizard of Oz* as I looked around the backyard and saw dust and sand whirling around in mini-tornadoes. I went into the house just as big drops of rain began to fall. The lightning was getting closer and closer, striking the desert floor in great forks that ran from the gray clouds to the ground. Because the pipe was at an angle, I was hoping not much rain would get in and that the kitten wouldn't drown. The storm lasted for an hour. By the time it ended and I went back outside, it was too dark to see into the pipe. I turned toward the house and a brilliant rainbow made an arc in the dark blue-gray sky over Eden. I stood on the front porch and saw the storm moving north—lightning still striking the ground and thunder rumbling. Every time the lightning struck, the telephone wires coming to the house hummed and crackled.

The next morning I went out to the pipe and hauled my shirt out of the hole. It was too dark to see in, but it didn't smell good so that was that. I untied the knots in my shirt and sobbed. An hour or so later, I saw a different kitten, the little gray-and-black one, slowly walking toward the back entryway where it had gone to hide in the corner of a canvas grill cover that hung from a peg on the wall. It walked slowly and its tail was down, almost dragging on the ground. I put some bits of turkey on a plate and a little spot of milk and put it under the grill cover. The kitten was just curled in a tight little ball in the corner with its eyes shut.

The odds are stacked against that kitten surviving. Great horned owls, red-tailed hawks, and golden eagles cruise the desert around Steve's house, and the kitten is defenseless against those raptors. This is where the harsh reality of the desert strikes home.

Now I look beyond the backyard and into miles of sagebrush desert and watch as the kitten disappears into it. I know Steve doesn't want a kitten here—he doesn't want that responsibility. One of his dogs could kill it with one quick shake of its head. I'm just determined to keep the kitten alive on my watch, probably because I couldn't save the other one. And who knows what happened to the third kitten—the black-and-white one I saw tumbling with the striped one out by the pigeon coop.

And all this has made me think—has kept me up at night, really, thinking about the nature of life and death in the desert. I can watch a falcon kill a sage grouse in a stoop and not feel anything but exhilaration at witnessing the dramatic flight, but I'm a blubbering mess and lose sleep about a kitten heading out into the desert. I guess that's because it just doesn't seem like a fair match. Life and death in the desert is a natural thing, and just under the serene-looking surface, it's happening all the time, if we choose to see it. But there's no parent guiding that kitten, showing it what to do. It has no peers. It's alone in a sea of sage with few defenses to keep it alive. It doesn't have the speed of a rabbit or even the smarts of a ground squirrel that knows enough to dive into a hole if something approaches. If it returns to the safety of the grill cover tonight, there will be a bowl of Alley Cat dry cat food that I bought at the feed store waiting.

I tell Steve about the kitten in a note and tell him I never, ever want to talk about it or hear what happened to it.

In the late afternoon I love to sit on the cabin's front porch. It's so quiet here, except for the wind rushing through the leaves of the Russian olive tree on the edge of the little front yard, which is big enough for a small croquet course. The front yard is delineated by a rail fence that Steve built—its uprights make an inverted V—and the rail fence is standing straight and tall in spite of the relentless Wyoming wind (Steve had figured out he had to bolt a cross brace across the bottom of the fence uprights).

Steve has an American flag and a Wyoming flag strung up on a pole at the end of the cabin, and they *thwack thwack* against the metal pole in the ever present wind. And as I sit there, I hear all the bird sounds—the *cheep*s and *squeak*s and *buzz*es and *coo*s and *cronk*s—and the noise of a very occasional truck, maybe two a day, that passes by the front of the house. I don't know where they're going because the road beyond the cabin just seems to stretch out into the desert. One day a helicopter was flying low across the back of Steve's property. Joe told me this is how they do seismographic survey work now, when they're looking at a new area for drilling. They fly people and equipment in because the BLM has a new rule that only established two-track roads that are marked on their map can be used. They'd been finding that the survey people were ripping up the desert doing their work.

The sprinkler system, which is set up in front of the cabin, goes on about five times a day. It is providing a haven for the birds and not the grass it was meant to water, since the grass seed never germinated. There are big muddy puddles that sit for about an hour between tufts of long grass—grass that preceded the seeding effort. If Steve doesn't watch out, the water will be drawing ducks in during migration. Maybe that's his plan. Birds sit under the spray of the sprinkler, wings spread, as they catch cool drops of water in the hot Wyoming sun. Swallows sit on the telephone and electric wires coming to the cabin from a pole a football field away by the washboard road. If I sit quietly, flycatchers hawking alfalfa moths from the air will come in and sit on the porch rail to eat their catch.

The buzzing of flies is sometimes broken by the deep thrum of a hummingbird coming in to inspect the sugar-water-filled feeder with its four big bright red plastic trumpet-vine flowers. The bird does a flyby, inspecting the feeder, then comes in to feed. One of them, distinguished from the others by a light band around its neck, gives a little chip note every time it stops in midair and then changes direction. Once a hummingbird commits to the feeder, it sits on the perch below the plastic flower. When it leans forward to dip its long beak into the flower, the wings come to its side, and when it leans back, the wings open up and rapidly fan back and forth. After about three dips like this, it settles down and just leans forward and back and seems to be at rest while letting the sweet water run down its throat. All this happens in a matter of seconds. Then it's on its way, usually to flit around the dusky green Russian olive tree.

Outside the fence is an intermediate section—not desert and not front yard—with patchy grass sprouting out of the taupe-colored gravel. Here the ground squirrels have created quite a village. They're like prairie dogs and seem very curious and will come out of their holes and sit up and look at me. Ravens fly low over this field, sending the squirrels scrambling, and occasionally I'll hear a loud buzzing that sounds like a supercharged peeper and then I'll see a harrier flying low across the field. One day I looked out and saw a big buck pronghorn in this no man's land, resting with his legs folded under him and his head up, looking around.

All day long flocks of ten to twenty pigeons fly around the cabin. Sometimes they light on the electrical wires, where they teeter in the wind, tails jerking up and down to help them stay upright. Sometimes they land in the front yard to get a drink of water; sometimes they wander around the gravelly backyard looking for who-knows-what in the sandy soil. They're white, and brown and white, and gray with bars, and gray and blue, and dark slate with white primaries.

Cottontails are everywhere—hopping, stopping, nibbling on the grass, then hopping some more. When I go to my car, there are always a number of them under it, grabbing the shade of the vehicle. Occasionally I'll see a jackrabbit, which looks long and gangly compared to the little bunnies.

A dozen sandhill cranes come in to feed in the alfalfa field next to the cabin. These huge, long-legged birds are four feet tall, and they breed west of the Great Lakes before migrating south. I know of only one pair of sandhill cranes in upstate New York, so I got pretty excited to see them, the same way people get excited to see great blue herons—which are common as dirt in my area—when they visit me. Joe said that there is a resident pair of cranes that have chicks every year. The mated pair stay together for life and migrate with their offspring. They hang around the field next to the cabin because the pickings are good in the alfalfa field and there's a pond about a quarter of a mile away.

The clouds start to build up in the late afternoon, and the wind picks up then as well. A meadowlark and a bird that looks like a small killdeer are getting a drink. I can see trucks moving on Highway 28 west of Farson, a ribbon of road identifiable by a heat shimmer about five miles away across the desert. They look like toy trucks. A brown grassland bird has come in—it has a white front with brown speckles and some white feathers are noticeable in its tail when it flies. It has a long tail that looks really long when the bird leans forward to drink and it sticks straight up. I later decide it's a sage thrasher.

Soon the clouds gather and cling together like bits of cotton being drawn into a loose pile. In no time they've created towering thunderheads. I hear distant thunder, and the flags *thwack thwack thwack* furiously against the metal pole. Lightning flashes in the northeast, and soon bolts of light strike the ground and ragged lines of light march across the desert to a thunder drum corps in front of the house, creating a dramatic display of light and sound. I wonder if the electricity will go out this time. The storm is violent and the wind whips the branches of the olive tree on the edge of the yard. The wind wants to tear the cushions from the willow chairs on the front porch and fling them about the desert, but Steve has secured the cushions to their wooden frames with bungee cords.

Then it's over just as quickly as it came up.

The last rays of a setting sun force themselves through the black clouds, and when I walk out into the backyard and look behind me toward the cabin, the wet red metal roof gleams and shines. A vivid rainbow arches through the dark gray sky and, looked at just right, seems to come straight out of the cabin's chimney. Or maybe those bands of light are sliding right down the chimney to a pot of gold hidden in the basement bunk-house.

By the back door sit a metal wheelbarrow and a large metal tub filled with things picked up in the desert, including rusty license plates, cans of all sizes, metal plates and pans, medicine bottles, milk bottles, wind-scoured pieces of ceramic dishes, bits of colored glass, skulls of pronghorn and deer, and maybe an antler or two. On the morning after the storm that killed the kitten, I found the wheelbarrow had tipped over, scattering the skulls and rusty pans in a ten-foot radius.

The back door is surrounded—completely surrounded—by desert-dried and sun-bleached antlers nailed to the doorjamb, creating a prickly, arch reminder that death happens.

Steve doesn't have many chances to make anything but a quick trip to the cabin during the summer because of his real job. He presents the bird show at Salt Lake City's Hogle Zoo—the same zoo where he'd befriended the zoo director decades before. He gives two shows a day, seven days a week. Rather than work as a zoo employee, Steve operates as an independent contractor. The birds he uses in the show—including macaws, pigeons, Harris's hawks, golden and bald eagles, an eagle owl, peregrines, European kestrels, barn owls, ferruginous hawks, red-tails, lanners, ravens, and cockatiels—are Steve's birds and are housed in his backyard or garage during the months when the bird show isn't being presented.

He's been in the bird-show business for the past twenty-eight years. It's the perfect occupation for a falconer who wants to spend most of the hunting season in the field, because, like the hunting, the work is seasonal. Steve believes it takes a fal-coner to run a bird show properly because falconers understand the kind of consistent training and strict adherence to routine that's necessary. It can be grueling work because it is so repetitive, and Steve's almost compulsive attention to detail means that he has a hard time delegating tasks.

Because Steve's been doing a bird show in Salt Lake City for so long—fourteen years at the Tracy Aviary, then fourteen years at the Hogle Zoo—he's attracted a real following. Kids grew up watching those birds fly, and Steve gets letters from people who have moved out of the area saying that when they come back to visit, they always come see the bird show. He especially likes it when these repeat customers recognize that he tries to make the show bigger and better every year. Steve knows that his future is in his own hands, and he makes sure his presentation is as good as it can be and in demand every year.

"It takes a lot of creative thinking to come up with the routines," said Steve. "The whole purpose of my show is basically to share my love of birds and to show how amazing they are. They really can think. They really do have personalities and an incredible ability to reason and figure things out."

I saw a couple of performances—held in an outdoor amphitheater at the zoo—and Steve is really good at it. The centerpiece is the free flights of the hawks over the crowd. Sometimes a hawk will come from behind the audience and swoop down over their heads before landing on a trainer's gloved fist. Other times it'll come from a box high atop a pole outside the amphitheater. Before the show, Steve places a hawk in the box at the base of a high pole then hoists the box up with a rope and pulley. During the show he cues the music, then uses a device like a garage-door opener to raise the front of the box; the hawk emerges and makes lazy circles in the sky, just like the song from *Oklahoma!* says it should. Then it lands on the edge of a big stick nest set on a platform on one side of the stage.

The script is fun and is delivered by either Steve or his right-hand man, Shawn, a young man in his midtwenties who started working with Steve as a volunteer a decade ago, when he was just a chubby-faced kid. At one point they send an African raven into the audience. It takes a dollar bill from a person's hand and then brings it back to a box where donations go to help a conservation project. In the past fourteen years, the bird show has brought in more than $100,000 for conservation. There's also a very cute bit in which Steve's daughter Jenna pretends to be an audience member and gets selected to come down front. Through a series of mishaps and a very funny exchange with her father, she ends up falling backward into a kiddie pool on the corner of the stage. Everyone looks shocked, then laughs nervously, then uproariously when it's revealed that Jenna works for the bird show.

At the end of each show, Steve and all the employees pose for photos with birds on their fists. I watched a mother and father lift a three-year-old onto the stage to pose with Steve, who was holding a bald eagle that was bigger than the kid. The kid looked terrified and started to cry. I told the parents I would be happy to take a picture of all of them so the kid could feel more comfortable sandwiched between his parents.

Although it's hard to believe today because Steve is such a polished showman—he understands the importance of rhythm and cadence and timing—he says he was really frightened to speak to the audiences when he started, almost three decades ago. He got a job feeding the birds at the Tracy Aviary, a city park with a little aviary, when he was in his early twenties, and soon he decided he wanted to make more out of the job and do something interesting. He trained about a dozen birds. Then he went around the park and gathered up some of the benches and arranged them for people to sit on while they watched the show. "I think that show basically turned the whole place around from being a little free park to a place where they started charging admission for the show before I left," said Steve. "The shows got so popular that a line would form at the admissions gate right before the starting time of the bird show." The way Steve sees it, he was able to share his love and appreciation of birds with people so they got a better understanding of them. But more important, it was a way for him to work during the spring and summer months only, leaving the fall and winter free for his falconry.

Working with birds his whole life means Steve has had his share of mishaps. Over the years he's had his hands severely bitten by parrots. He used to think you could get a parrot to stop biting you by acting as if you weren't afraid of it, but he found out that wasn't such a good idea. It made more sense to become their friend and try to read their moods. He learned that if a parrot is in a bad mood, you shouldn't put your hand near it. Steve said, "People come by, and it's almost instinctive—most people when they see a parrot in a cage say *Hi* and put their hand up, and the parrot goes *whomp*. I've learned that if they're going to bite you, you've got to think fast and just give them the back of your hand or your fist because they can't grab on and bite it."

Steve had a tame hyacinth macaw in the show that liked him but didn't like other people. He found that if a macaw likes you and someone strange comes near you, the macaw will bite you because of misplaced aggression. It really wants to bite the other person, but it bites you instead. "Well, I had this macaw and I was kind of showing off to show how tame and cute he was. So he came up to give me a kiss—that's where he puts that big black tongue out and he puts his tongue on your tongue to give you a kiss—only this time he chomped down and about split my tongue in half," said Steve. "My tongue swelled up so big I could barely get a straw in my mouth to sip juice. I don't do that anymore."

He learned some valuable lessons about cleaning the cages of the really big birds, such as the fact that vultures vomit when they're stressed. Steve's been vomited on by turkey, king, and hooded vultures and has learned not to clean their pens when the vultures have any food in them because they will vomit all over him.

Then there was the time he was in an Andean condor pen and had short pants on. This particular Andean condor male was so strong that when Steve put the lawn mower into the large pen to mow the lawn, that condor could start the mower by grabbing the rubber handle and pulling it. He found out that nothing can bite like a condor, which in the wild can bite through the toughest hide. Steve, of course, had thought the condor liked him, and he wasn't being particularly cautious. The bird charged at him, bit him on his inner thigh, and tore his pants off. It looked as if he'd been bit right in the crotch. As he was bleeding profusely, he realized that there were a bunch of people watching, horrified. That, he said, was the most serious bird bite he ever had. He had to have stitches.

Steve has done some commercial and movie work as a bird trainer, and often the production people want him to handle one of his eagles. For one movie, the director had him flying an eagle, but he didn't want the bird to have jesses on because they hung down so noticeably while it flew. So the director was doing take after take, and the eagle was starting to get pissed off. All of a sudden it came after Steve. He ran, dodged it, and hit the ground, and then he tried to get the bird to calm down. "I know a lot more about eagles now than I did then," he told me. "You never call an imprint eagle to your glove, you just throw the food on the ground and let it eat and then go over and pick it up." But this was before Steve knew that, and so he'd put his glove out and held the food and had the eagle eating on his fist when suddenly it reached right up and grabbed Steve's face with its talons. Steve tried to get loose, and the blood was everywhere. The director took one look and yelled, "That's a wrap."

After Steve washed up, he didn't look too bad because the talons hadn't gone in really deep. It didn't hang on, he said. It had just footed him in the face.

Another time, Steve was flying an eagle for a local bank's commercial, and the director wanted an eagle without jesses to soar across a canyon just as the sun was coming up on a beautiful winter day. Steve put the eagle way over on the side of the mountain, came back, and then called it to him. It flew just fine. The director said they needed another take so Steve set the eagle over there again, came back, and called it across. The big bird took a couple of circles over the canyon, which looked beautiful, and all of a sudden a wild golden eagle came flying through and chased Steve's bird. Steve's eagle flew off and sat in the top of a pine tree across the canyon where the wild eagle repeatedly dived at it. Luckily Steve had seen where it landed because there was no telemetry on the bird.

But there was a lot of snow on the ground. A lot of snow. It was well above his waist, and he had a hell of a time trying to wade through it as he made his way to the mountain. He finally got to the tree the eagle was in, and for some reason he left his gear at the bottom of the tree while he climbed up to the bird. As he neared the bird he thought it was getting spooky and acting as if it were about to fly, so Steve showed it some food, which seemed to upset the bird. Steve could tell it was getting ready to launch so he reached out and grabbed the eagle by one leg. "I only had hold of one leg and I knew he was going to try to beat the crap out of me. I didn't want to get it in the wrist so I pulled him in and before I knew what happened he got me in the meat of my thigh with his other foot and I just screamed bloody murder. I managed to get a hold of both feet with my hand and pulled him out of my thigh. It was horrible. My leg looked like I had been shot by a machine gun. There were big holes everywhere. Somehow I climbed out of the pine tree, holding the eagle by the feet with one hand.

When I got down to where I had left my stuff I hooded him and put jesses on him." Then he gave a sigh and added, "That was bad."

When Steve stays in the cabin in the summer, he drives around looking for broods of sage grouse. He's gotten some great photographs and video footage of the hens with their young as they move through the desert foraging for succulent young plants. He also drives on the two-tracks and checks out the barbed-wire fence line looking for evidence that grouse have hit it. Over the past several years he's walked along several fences that run through traditional grouse wintering areas, checking the barbs on the top strand for evidence of grouse strikes. He looks for little clumps of feathers stuck to a barb—he might find just one downy feather—but sometimes he'll find part of a wing. If he finds something, he looks around for a grouse carcass on the ground near the fence. He usually finds a little pile of feathers and maybe some bones, which is all that's left after the ravens and coyotes get through with the bird. These strikes are likely to happen far away from the fence posts; the grouse can see those when it's flying, but if it's flying low and fast, chances are it won't see a single strand of wire until it's too late and it plows right into it.

Steve keeps a tally of the number and location of grouse strikes he finds and submits the information to Wyoming Game and Fish. He's finally gotten their regional office in Green River interested in marking fences to protect the birds, and they're starting to throw a little money and time at the project. Over the past couple of years, Steve has marked some of the fences that have the most strikes himself; he attaches flattened aluminum cans hanging from a wire to the fence's top strand so the cans will dangle and swing in the wind, making the barbed wire noticeable to the flying birds. In the places where he's hung the cans, he hasn't seen any evidence of bird strikes, so he knows his method works.

"Wow, that's a lot of work," I said to Steve one day after going out to hang cans with him. He said he'll do anything to prevent the grouse from being killed unnecessarily. Of course he loves the sage grouse—I don't think there's a person alive who has spent as much time as he has observing them in the field, on the wing, and in the hand. In a way, it's paradoxical—he really loves what he kills. And he wants to maintain as high a population of sage grouse as possible so that when talk of listing those birds as threatened or endangered comes up, he knows that at least he did his part to try to save them. Maybe it's a form of penance.

13

Jonah Field

JOE HARMER AND I headed north up Route 191 toward Pinedale to visit the Jonah Field on a day so hot and hazy that
from Farson we could barely see the outline of the Wind River
Range. I'd invited Joe to come on the drive with me because, in
addition to being a local falconer, he was supplementing his re-
tirement income by working for a subcontractor who strapped
tanks—that is, measured the amount of oil or gas in them—for
the oil and gas industry. They drove to oil and gas fields between Colorado and North Dakota to strap tanks, and then sent
the figures to the oil companies, who used the information to
determine the rate of flow and capacity from a particular well. I
figured Joe would be useful in explaining what I was looking at
in the Jonah Field.

The Jonah natural gas field is tapping into one of the largest
pockets of natural gas in this country. The Jonah Field and the
adjacent Pinedale Anticline lie under the Upper Green River
Valley, an area known for its beauty as well as its natural resources. At present, there are about 3,500 wells drilled between
Pinedale and Farson, and there are plans to drill 35,000 wells in
an area from Pinedale all the way down to Rock Springs, about
ninety miles away. So far the drilling's pretty much confined to
the west side of Highway 191, and you can't see much activity
from the road. Joe said originally they were not going to drill

on the east side of the highway between Pinedale and Highway 28 going east from Farson, but on our way north to the Jonah Field we saw the beginnings of development—some new roads and a well or two.

I've driven to Pinedale several times and have looked for the Jonah Field from the road. North of Farson the topography changes, and the flat desert cut by gullies and creeks gives way to undulating hills. As I scanned the area I expected to see an industrial landscape. As I neared Pinedale, I saw some wells off in the distance—they looked like little cell-phone towers or mini-derricks—but that was about it.

I wanted to visit the Jonah Field because I knew its presence was changing the dynamic of southwestern Wyoming both environmentally and culturally. The whole area was experiencing a real economic boom because of natural gas exploration and extraction. Towns near the gas fields were expanding rapidly—housing, even temporary housing, was at a premium, and man camps, or supervised company housing for nonlocal gas workers, had sprung up. Everywhere you went, you saw evidence of the gas fields in the amount of traffic on the roads, the jacked-up prices for food, and the high ratio of men to women in the grocery stores, gas stations, and diners.

More important was the effect of these gas fields on the landscape and the sage grouse habitat. Most people who look across the desert see a barren place capable of supporting sagebrush and maybe a few head of cattle. But I was starting to see the high desert the way Steve saw it. What others saw as a harsh-looking landscape, I was beginning to see as fragile yet dynamic. Because no one had paid much attention to the area until recently, ruts from tens of thousands of wagons traveling along the Mormon and Oregon trails were still visible even a hundred and fifty years after they'd rolled through. Sagebrush a foot or two high was everywhere, and these plants—because they're so slow growing—could have been almost a century old.

Arrowheads and spear points dropped thousands of years ago still lay on the desert floor. Like the art of falconry, which has a timeless quality about it, the desert also seemed timeless—as if what we see today is the same thing the pioneers saw, and the Indians saw before them.

And looking just a little closer, like Steve does, I could see the sage grouse and the snakes and the rabbits. And the pronghorn and the elk and the wild horses. And the prairie falcons and the ferruginous hawks and the golden eagles. And if the niche for any one of these species is disturbed, it throws everything else out of whack. It made me wonder what Jomo and Jahanna see when they fly a thousand feet above Steve. Do they see the compressor stations and the ever expanding spider web of roads cutting through the desert? Do they see houses suddenly appearing where the desert had been scraped clean by large machines? Do they see fewer sage grouse?

Joe and I turned off the highway onto a wide washboard road at mile marker 67. There were a dozen small signs—the size of real estate signs—attached to the fence near the highway, each bearing the name of a different company, like En-Cana and BP. I guess it was to signal trucks and workers that this was indeed the place. About two hundred yards from the entrance, the wide two-lane washboard road spread out to four lanes to accommodate a couple of porta-potties and a parking area. We drove about a quarter of a mile farther up the road to the Jonah Field headquarters. Pickup trucks filled the parking lots surrounding two huge metal buildings. A high chainlink fence defined the perimeter. Joe said everyone who works on the site first has to come to the headquarters to watch a safety video that demonstrates important things such as how to run like hell into the wind if there's an explosion or fire. There are windsocks at almost every set of tanks to show which way the wind is blowing.

We then headed north into the natural gas field. As we drove we talked about what this place used to be like. This used to be one of Steve's favorite winter hunting areas because it contained the largest wintering ground of sage grouse in the county. It's also directly in the path of the longest migration of pronghorn in North America—up to fifty thousand of these ungulates migrate about two hundred miles from their summer range in Yellowstone to their winter range; the path takes them right through the Jonah Field. This is the second longest migration of mammals in North America—the longest being the caribou migration in Alaska. Because Steve assigns his own name to falconry locations, he called this area the White Rainbow wintering grounds.

As we drove on, obeying the thirty-five-mile-an-hour speed limit, which wasn't difficult because of the frequent potholes, we started to see some gas wells. Joe explained what we were looking at: "There's a well that's already up and running . . . over there they're staking out the area to pour the concrete pad . . . over there they're digging a pond and lining it with thick black plastic because they're preparing to frac the well. That's where they force sand and water into the well to fracture the cracks containing the natural gas and then they leave the sand behind and pump the water out . . . this here is a compressor station where they make the oil or natural gas or condensate flow more efficiently through the pipeline. And don't ask me what condensate is because I don't know."

In the mid-1990s engineers figured out how to extract the previously unextractable natural gas that lay trapped in millions of bubbles in sandstone ten to twelve thousand feet below the surface of the Jonah Field. By forcing a slurry of water and gravel into a well hole, engineers could fracture the layers that trapped the gas, and the gravel would keep these fractures open and allow the gas to escape into the piping leading to the surface. The water would then be pumped out and put into a holding pond. This innovation, coupled with rising gas and oil

prices—natural gas prices have quadrupled in the past decade—and a desire for less dependence on foreign markets, led to
Wyoming's recent oil and gas boom. EnCana says eight trillion
cubic feet of natural gas lie under the Jonah Field. With a two-
billion-dollar budget surplus from gas royalties in 2006 alone,
state and local coffers have become flush. Per capita income in
Wyoming rose 43 percent from 2000 to 2006, the largest increase in the nation. The state eliminated sales tax on groceries
and created scholarships for state colleges. The little town of
Pinedale, population about 1,600, lies just to the north of the
Jonah Field. It has so much money that the citizens are running out of wish-list projects to fund—they have their hockey
rink, an aquatic center, a new community center, and a senior
center. The school recently gave each fifth-grader a brand-new
laptop computer, and teachers' salaries have doubled in the
past four years.

In order to really understand the impact of oil and gas on
the state, you have to look at property rights, which have always been complicated in the West. Layers upon layers of rights
are involved in drilling for gas, some real and some perceived.
First, someone holds the subsurface rights to the land, and this
may or may not be the landowner. If the landowner owns the
rights to both the surface and subsurface, it's called full estate.
If someone owns just the subsurface rights or just the surface
rights, it's called split estate. Full-estate landowners can make
a good living from the royalties from wells on their land. Full-
estate ranchers in gas-producing areas in Wyoming had hit on
hard times with the fall in beef prices, but suddenly they could
make a decent living from natural gas royalties, which can range
from virtually nothing to about $100,000 per year. However,
split-estate ranchers who own just the surface rights are forced
to stand by and watch as oil and gas companies who hold subsurface rights bulldoze paths and put in roads and create well
pads and slurry ponds without regard to property lines. Often

a one-time payment is made to the rancher to compensate for some of his loss, but this kind of incursion onto someone's land, particularly in the West, leaves a really bad taste in a landowner's mouth.

In Wyoming, to date, about 95 percent of the drilling has occurred on federal lands. On BLM land, the federal government holds the subsurface rights, which they in turn lease to oil and gas companies, who then have the right to develop these parcels. Under George W. Bush, the federal government eased the environmental and developmental restrictions on more than sixty million acres in the West—a couple million of those acres are in Sublette County, Wyoming, site of the Jonah Field—which led to a 70 percent increase in the number of drilling permits issued on BLM land. But the government also leases the surface grazing rights to local landowners and allows recreational use of the land and hunting during hunting seasons. There have been competing interests for land in the West forever, including settlers versus Native Americans, farmers versus ranchers, hunters versus ranchers, development versus wilderness, and invasive species versus native species. This most recent round of natural gas exploration is just putting pressure on an already uneasy détente among the special interests. And all involved invoke the "preservation of the western way of life," whatever that means, when lobbying for their interests, whether they're sheepherders or cowboys or ranchers or Indians or oil company executives. The question "What is the western way of life and how can all these interests coexist and still preserve it?" is worth trying to answer.

Besides bringing money into the state and the small towns, natural gas exploration is bringing an influx of people. Oilfield workers from as far away as Texas and Louisiana have come north in search of high-paying jobs. A foreman can earn $150,000 a year, and a worker in the fields can get twenty-eight dollars an hour and all the overtime he can handle. Man camps have sprung up outside of Big Piney and Pinedale and even Farson, and there's a severe housing shortage in the area; developments are being mapped out and houses built as quickly as contractors can put them up. The average price of a house in Pinedale has almost doubled in the past couple of years.

Another unintended consequence of the natural gas boom is the drain of workers from local communities like Pinedale. Every single able-bodied person who can get a job in the oil fields has done so, which leaves the little restaurants and gas stations and grocery stores desperate for help. Even though the average wage for jobs in town is thirteen dollars an hour, the local businesses are begging for employees. The TrueValue Hardware store had to close last year because it couldn't get affordable help. Things are so out of balance that there are almost twenty real estate offices in Pinedale but only a couple of places to eat. A brand-new AmeriHost Pinedale Inn has opened up on the far end of town. They advertise themselves as "oil-field friendly" and the eighty-two rooms are booked for the foreseeable future. Although the town's residents are grateful for the infusion of money into what had been a depressed area, they're growing weary of the extra people. They've also seen a marked increase in crime, and law enforcement is stretched thin. It's as if the community's shell-shocked by the whole thing. There's a methamphetamine problem in the region, and cops are discovering meth labs where people are cooking up the stuff for the oil-field workers. There was a recent item in the Pinedale newspaper reporting that ten to twelve dogs had gone missing in southwest Wyoming and the animal-control people were wondering if they had been stolen for methamphetamine testing or for dog fighting—two things you don't want to have happen in your neighborhood. This part of Wyoming has gotten a little wilder and frontier-like in the past couple of years.

About a week before Joe and I visited the Jonah Field, I took a drive from the cabin to Pinedale. I went because I wanted to buy a book, but I also went because it was so hot that I felt as if the rubber would melt off my sneakers if I spent any time outside. I knew the sixty-mile drive to Pinedale guaranteed a hundred and twenty miles of relative comfort in an air-conditioned car. As always, I looked for signs of the natural gas fields and saw a couple of derricks off in the distance. A more immediate reminder was the constant stream of truck traffic on Route 191—huge tanker trucks, trucks hauling earthmoving equipment, tricked-out pickup trucks carrying men going to and from the oil fields. There was also the occasional camper or family car loaded with bored kids and vacation stuff, clearly making the western rounds.

A few days earlier I had been having a late lunch at Mitch's Café when one of these families came in and sat at the big round table in the corner. The sullen teenage girl played with a cell phone and listened to an iPod, and the younger boy was glued to some kind of Game Boy. The mother was beautiful in a Connecticut kind of way, with lovely hair and lovely clothes and a perfect smile showing her perfect teeth. The father had a sweater draped over his shoulders, the sleeves knotted in front, and wore khaki shorts, a polo shirt, and deck shoes with socks. And because the father was probably an ad executive in New York, he was charming and kidded the waitress about the hot sauce and asked her about the road to Jackson Hole. They ordered a ton of food, ate about a third of it, and dropped a pile of money on the table. Quite a contrast to the table of four oil-field workers in their dirty T-shirts, blue jeans, and work boots, and the couple of old ranchers with their big cowboy hats and long-sleeved shirts with snaps up the front and on the breast pockets who sat in the corner and good-naturedly harassed the waitress. They were like a microcosm of the West—the family from the East is here to see the iconic West, which was created in part by the old ranchers and which is being systematically changed by the oil men.

As I neared Pinedale that hot afternoon, the first thing I noticed were the brand-new housing developments marching up the hills on the outskirts of town. When I reached town I saw that I had stumbled upon the Green River Rendezvous weekend, which was both good and bad. The four- or five-block-long Pine Street had tables and booths set up along the sidewalks, and people wearing either Native American costumes or Mountain Man garb were hawking everything from beaded jewelry to T-shirts to bowie knives. Even though it was about 105 degrees in the shade, Mountain Men sauntered down the street in full buckskin attire—leather pants and shirts with fringes, some kind of animal-skin hats on their heads, knives strapped to their legs with leather laces, and leather boots on their feet. I thought I would faint from heat exhaustion just looking at them. I guess I had just missed the big parade, and people were streaming down a side street to watch rodeo events and visit a Mountain Man encampment.

Faler's, the low-slung grocery-hardware-gift-liquor store—truly one-stop shopping—was full of people who'd come in hoping to beat the heat, a mistake because Faler's didn't have air conditioning, just big fans moving the hot air around. I passed a Mountain Man in one aisle scrutinizing the brands of potato chips and another in the produce section eyeing the apples. I waited in line to buy a Coke behind a Mountain Man with a bad sunburn on the part of his face not covered by a wispy gray beard. He held his leather hat in his hand and fanned himself, sending a pungent musky odor of leather and sweat my way. "Hot day," he said as he pushed more air toward his face with his hat.

Up the hill behind Faler's was the Mountain Man Museum, and this was its big weekend. Adjacent to the museum a small Indian encampment of tepees and a sweat lodge had sprung up. One of the tepees was a traditional brain-tanned, sinew-sewn buffalo-hide tepee—a faithful re-creation of a Plains Indian tepee.

The Green River Rendezvous has been taking place in or near Pinedale since the 1830s (with a hundred-year hiatus between 1836 and 1936) and is always on the second weekend in July. The original rendezvous were gatherings of fur trappers (AKA mountain men), traders, and Indians. Trappers spent most of the year in isolation as they traveled through the mountains and the rivers of the West in search of pelts, particularly beaver pelts. There seemed to be an inexhaustible demand for beaver pelts in Europe, where beaver hats were all the rage. There also seemed to be an inexhaustible supply of the mammals in the clear lakes and rivers of the West.

Once a year the trappers and traders agreed to meet—or rendezvous—at a particular time and place. For six years in the early 1830s, that place was just below the Green River, near the site of modern-day Pinedale. What became known as the Green River Rendezvous were rowdy, raucous affairs replete with trading, drinking, whoring, fighting, and swapping of tall tales. John C. Frémont, Jim Bridger, Jedediah Smith, and Kit Carson came to one or more of the Green River Rendezvous. They would all go on to find fame in American history texts for exploring, mapping, and guiding people through unknown regions of the West. Then, rather abruptly, trappers realized the rivers, streams, and lakes were being tapped out, and they had to push farther and farther west to find beaver. At about the same time, European fashion changed and beaver hats were no longer in demand. Like many people in the history of the West, trappers found they had to adapt and change their way of life, and many former mountain men went on to guide wagon trains full of settlers on their way to the promise of free or cheap land in the far West.

I thought about the legacy of the mountain men as I pushed through crowds of faux Mountain Men on the sidewalks of Pinedale. And because my thoughts were never far from Steve, I threw the mantle of modern-day Mountain Man around him, and it fit him like a pair of leather pants after a rainstorm. Like these western predecessors, Steve could exist only in a particular place at a particular time. He had to have the right kind of falcons to hunt the right kind of game in the right kind of habitat, much like the mountain men who'd found themselves in the right place at the right time. And these rugged individuals separated by almost two hundred years are dependent upon the capriciousness and whims of others. In the case of the mountain men, their livelihood was dictated by the fashion whims of men thousands of miles away. When European men's fashion tastes shifted to the Orient and silk, the mountain men in the West found themselves without jobs. In Steve's case, events beyond his control—a war in Iraq, a new technology for extracting hard-to-get natural gas, America's continually expanding lust for energy, and spiraling gas prices—combined to speed the sage grouse toward extinction. Like the mountain men before him, Steve will have his good years when the sky is the limit, but before he knows it, it will be over. The gas wells will intrude too far on the mating and nesting habits of the grouse, and the habitat will be too badly fragmented to sustain a large enough population of birds to permit hunting. And then the government will list them as threatened, and that will be that.

I never did find a bookstore in Pinedale on that hot day in July. I made my way down to the other end of town and went into the oil-field-friendly AmeriHost Pinedale Inn, where a desk clerk told me there wasn't a bookstore in town. "Used to be a place that sold books," she said. "But it closed." And I wondered why the hell a place with all that money to burn couldn't keep a bookstore in business.

As Joe and I drove through the Jonah Field, we started seeing wells here and there, which led me to think it wasn't so bad, but soon we got to an area where there were well pads and tanks and roads covering the high-desert floor on the hills and in the draws; where there was no sagebrush left at all; where it was clear that this area would not support any wildlife any time soon. In places where there was a high density of activity, the area had been scraped clean of vegetation, and in a high-desert region with little rainfall and extremely slow-growing plants, the land would be scraped clean for a long time. We saw pronghorn walking through the gas fields, apparently undisturbed by what was going on around them. We drove past a sign announcing Loose Stock Area, meaning ranchers were also running cattle here because, goddamn it, they held the grazing rights.

A steady stream of trucks ranging in size from pickups to double tankers drove past us on the road through the Jonah Field. At one point we passed a well being drilled very near the road; seven or eight trailers, each with its own satellite dish, were parked next to the well pad. Joe said these were for the workers who worked seven days on and then went home for a few days. Reminded me of a bunker program for a fire station or the setup that tugboat captains have at Pilottown down by mile marker 1 in the Mississippi River. When you're on, you're on. Everything is full-bore in the gas fields, twenty-four hours a day, seven days a week.

After miles and miles of this I was ready to turn around, and as we headed back the way we came I saw a buck pronghorn standing near the road, looking down into a valley that was choked with wells. It was as if he were considering what lay before him. At the foot of the little draw was a windmill—not the new kind, with the big airplane propeller, but the kind you often see in the rural West; the kind that ranchers put in years ago to draw nice cool water from the earth for their cattle; the small wooden kind that make us reach for our cameras because we look at them and recognize the symbols of the disappearing West. The windmill was surrounded by well pads and tanks and derricks in different stages of completion. It reminded me that Americans have always tried to exploit the natural resources of an area, mainly because we can. Joe frequently said that all those environmentalists and liberals who drive into the Jonah Field in their big SUVs to take pictures would be crying a different story if they had to give up their electricity or their vehicles. "Ninety percent of the people would die in the first year if they couldn't have fossil fuels," he said. He doesn't want to hear any of their bitching.

I slowed down and pulled over, scaring off six ravens picking at a carcass on the side of the road. I got out, took a look, and yelled to Joe that it was a sage grouse. I had seen the dead bird on the way in and said it looked like a grouse but Joe had said no way. The bird had clearly gotten hit by a truck and was now raven food. Perfect example of one of the dangers of the gas field for the sage grouse: the ones who don't get scared away by the noise and the lights have to navigate the spider web of roads that crisscross their habitat. I remember reading a quote from an EnCana spokesman who said that the reality with oil and gas is that they drill holes where the gas is, and, unfortunately, in this part of Wyoming, that happens to be in sage grouse habitat. But he went on to assure people that although there would be disturbances to the habitat, they could manage it and stay ahead of the problems. EnCana is a Calgary-based company with hundreds and hundreds of wells in the Jonah Field—they drilled almost four hundred new wells between 2003 and 2007.

Trying to interpret the current literature about what sage grouse need to survive is like stepping through Alice's looking glass. *Yeah, that sounds right,* I think as I read one report, then the next report says the exact opposite. What's real is false and what's false is real. One report says the sage grouse population is as healthy as ever, and the next one says they're poised on the brink of extinction. An unpublished industry report says the birds can survive with as many as eight wells per square mile. The work done by University of Wyoming graduate student

Matt Holloran says that that number has to be as low as one well per square mile. The U.S. Fish and Wildlife Service says that oil and gas represents the single greatest threat to the sage grouse but they can't really pinpoint how or why this development affects the birds. They're even sketchy about the numbers of birds there are, and estimate the population at somewhere between 150,000 and 500,000 spread across a seven-state area. In June 2007, Wyoming governor David Freudenthal hosted a two-day summit about the sage grouse, bringing together academics, policymakers, and industry representatives to try to make sense of the data and come up with a plan for preserving the bird.

In 2005 the U.S. Fish and Wildlife Service rejected a plan to list the sage grouse under the Endangered Species Act, but that decision was challenged in the courts by Western Watersheds Project. A federal district judge ruled that the agency ignored expert advice and allowed improper political interference when it decided to deny federal protection to the sage grouse. The judge found that former Interior Department official Julie McDonald used overt pressure and intimidation tactics and edited scientific conclusions to keep the birds from being listed. The U.S. Fish and Wildlife Service has to review the plan again.

In June 2008 the Theodore Roosevelt Conservation Partnership and the North American Grouse Partnership asked the federal government to impose new restrictions on oil and gas development in order to protect the sage grouse. They contend that BLM and the Department of the Interior are ignoring peer-reviewed science that shows sage grouse breeding areas are suffering as a result of rapid oil and gas development. One thing they're proposing is that the required buffer between oil and gas drilling and sage grouse leks be extended from a quarter of a mile to two miles.

Whatever happens with listing or not listing the sage grouse, this is a fight that isn't going to go away any time soon. Some companies are offering to mitigate the disruption of habitat by setting aside other parcels of sagebrush, which is a great idea if the grouse happen to be there. But no one really knows what happens to grouse that are forced from their traditional areas. Can you force grouse from one region and hope they find the set-aside sagebrush? So far, the research shows them to be extremely site specific with regard to leks—breeding grounds—and wintering areas.

There are six gas companies operating in the Jonah Field right now, and they are subject to a ruling that says that only 46 percent of the 30,500-acre field can be disturbed at any given time. This includes pipelines, roads, well pads, and any other infrastructure. When that threshold is reached, land must be reclaimed to a functioning ecosystem before more acreage is disturbed. This disturbance area is being tracked and monitored via satellite imagery and reviewed on a quarterly basis.

Steve doesn't drive up into the White Rainbow wintering ground anymore because it's too depressing, and if he doesn't see it, he doesn't have to think about it too often. He submitted written comments for the original environmental impact statement that was required before any of the wells were drilled. In his letter he wrote about the sage grouse wintering grounds occupied by hundreds and hundreds of birds and about flying falcons in those beautiful arroyos and rounded hills. What he got for his efforts was a couple of gas wells nicknamed Falcon 1 and Falcon 2.

14

Sage Grouse

IN DECEMBER 2007 Wyoming governor Dave Freudenthal brought together a group of experts in the field of wildlife management and mapping to discuss what to do about the sage grouse. Freudenthal made no bones about the fact that listing the sage grouse as threatened or endangered would have huge and painful consequences for the state. He told the *Casper Tribune,* "This is very serious, because if you look at the map of sage grouse habitat in Wyoming, it covers a lot of the state. If the sage grouse is listed in Wyoming, it could have a very serious impact on the way we hunt and recreate, and how we develop the state's natural resources."

The December meeting was convened just days after the U.S. district judge's ruling that U.S. Fish and Wildlife had to reconsider its decision about whether to list the bird as threatened or endangered under the Endangered Species Act. During the previous summer, the governor's office had created a statewide Sage Grouse Implementation Team to "provide guidance for implementing strategies that enhance sagebrush ecosystems in varying stages of life form, age, and condition throughout Wyoming . . . the ultimate goal is to stabilize and increase sage-grouse populations." The top priority for the team is to map the bird's distribution in the state. Only then can they look at the habitat and figure out which activities, including oil and gas and housing development, have the most impact.

The governor, hunters, ranchers, and companies involved in energy exploration and mineral extraction are desperate to keep the sage grouse from being listed under the Endangered Species Act. Originally, the sage grouse population was around sixteen million, according to estimates, and flocks of this large bird once darkened the skies of sixteen western states and three Canadian provinces. Today they can be found in just seven states—with two stronghold populations anchored in Wyoming—and maybe a couple of Canadian provinces. This is not a sexy bird; it's big and grayish brown with a black belly and white neck feathers. Its mottled gray-brown feathers speckled with white are designed to help it blend into its surroundings. The sage grouse is, however, an iconic bird of the high desert, and its range has decreased by almost half, primarily because of habitat degradation. More important, its numbers may be down to an estimated 140,000 birds—about 9 percent of presumed historic levels. And most of the birds that are left live on public land and are at the mercy of federal and state public land management agencies, like the Bureau of Land Management and the U.S. Forest Service—agencies that attempt to please ranchers, hunters, and energy companies.

In July of 2000, the Wyoming Sage Grouse Working Group was formed to develop a statewide strategy for the conservation of sage grouse in Wyoming. The working group consists of eighteen Wyoming citizens from a range of backgrounds, including agricultural, industrial, governmental, environmental, hunting, and Native American tribal interests. To date, the state has managed to keep the bird from being listed. However, there is a great deal of pressure to list the species as threatened or endangered, and if this happens, the consequences will be felt by everyone from the owners of energy companies that hold

the mineral rights and relentlessly drill for natural gas on public lands to the ranchers who own the grazing rights and run
their cattle on public lands to the gun hunter and the falconer
who hunt sage grouse on public lands. Everyone knows that in
order to save this bird, critical habitat must be preserved and
restored.

The male greater sage grouse (*Centrocercus urophasianus*)
is a good-looking bird during the breeding season, but, except
for hunters, wildlife enthusiasts, and land managers, most people don't really think about the species. It's not really the kind
of bird anyone would notice when driving through Wyoming
on Route 191, although one of these big birds might be standing
within sight of the road. It doesn't have the pizzazz of a pheasant or the cuteness of a California quail. It doesn't have the long
neck of a wild turkey, although it does have its heft. And it's
unlikely to be profiled on the state's license plate. Completely
dependent on sagebrush for food and cover, sage grouse rarely
stray far from the plants. But like an injured ruffed grouse Steve
found on the road in Emigration Canyon when he was a kid—a
bird that made Steve realize the beauty and complexity of the
coloration of a bird's feathers—sage grouse have a subtle beauty
that is more evident when the bird is in the hand rather than in
the bush. The male, or cock, birds can reach eight pounds—a
staggering weight when you consider that falconers hunt sage
grouse with hybrids weighing a fifth of that. Despite their large
size and chunky build, sage grouse are powerful flyers that
rocket across the gray sagebrush desert reaching seventy miles
an hour in their long, straight flights.

In March of each year and continuing until June, cock
birds gather in communal leks—areas of competitive mating
display—where they strut and show off for the hens for several
hours at the end of each day. These spectacular displays attract
hens that come to watch the gathering of toughs—like coeds
going to a singles bar—and they watch as the males spread the

feathers of their long, normally spiky tails and fluff out their white neck feathers to form huge ruffs that surround their heads. Then two air sacs on the cock bird's chest fill and deflate and turn a bright orange-red as air passes in and out of them. The weird sounds they make—something like the glugging sounds kids make when they're pretending to gag—can be heard up to a mile away from a lek of dozens of strutting male birds. This noise is also called booming, hence the nickname "boomer" for a big cock bird. Hens wander around the edges of the strutting pack and try to choose the sexiest male to mate with. Ultimately, only one or at most a couple of the males in the lek will mate with all the females, so the stakes are high for the male hopefuls.

After mating, that's the end of male involvement in sage grouse family life. The female flies off to choose a nesting spot, which can be anywhere from an adjacent stretch of thick sagebrush to a sagebrush plant six miles from the lek. She builds a nest on the ground under a sagebrush bush or in a thick clump of grass. The nest is a shallow depression lined with a bit of plant material. In it she lays seven to nine eggs, which hatch about twenty-six days later. Shortly after hatching, the downy young are able to leave the nest to find food on their own, although the female continues to tend them. At first the chicks eat mostly insects—ants, bees, wasps, grasshoppers, and beetles. They gradually add the leaves and buds of plants such as prairie dandelion, milk vetch, prickly lettuce, and evening primrose to their diet. Adult birds live almost exclusively on the leaves of sagebrush, particularly big sagebrush, silver sagebrush, threetip sagebrush, low sagebrush, and black sagebrush. Sage grouse eggs and young birds face many threats to survival, not the least of which are coyotes, ravens, raptors, and cattle, which sometimes trample them.

During the fall, sage grouse move into habitats containing both sagebrush and grassland—often found on the edges of agricultural fields—and they increase their consumption of sagebrush relative to other plants. The nonbreeding females and males stay separate until the weather turns cold, and then they gather in large winter flocks. In winter, access to sagebrush is critical, since it provides both food and cover in the snow. These big dark-colored birds blend in beautifully with the sage but can look terribly exposed when caught out in the open. Preferred winter habitat is characterized by big sagebrush plants that rise above the snow so the birds can use them as roosts as well as food. The timing of winter migration, or the gathering of the winter flocks, depends on the arrival of snow, and winter ranges may vary from year to year depending on the cover and depth of the snow.

No one really knows how much sagebrush habitat is necessary to support viable populations of sage grouse. Some groups of sage grouse are nonmigratory; some may travel a dozen miles between summer and winter ranges; and yet others may make annual migrations of forty-five miles or more. The home range of migratory sage grouse can exceed 575 square miles.

Threats to sage grouse populations are numerous. In areas where there is mineral extraction and natural gas exploration, the sage grouse habitat is degraded and fragmented by roads, pipelines, wells, compressor stations, and mines. Power lines that snake along roads leading to mining or drilling operations provide convenient places for raptors to perch on and hunt from. Evaporation ponds contain undrinkable water that's been pumped from wells. In places where water has been forced out of the earth during coal-bed methane extraction, the water table is lowered. This alters the aboveground landscape, leading to fewer and different plants. Noise and dust from all the activity disturbs the birds, particularly during the breeding season, when they depend on being able to hear one another. In areas where cattle graze, applications of herbicides to encourage the growth of fodder for cattle has led to the destruction of large swaths of sagebrush. Although pesticides may be of low toxicity to birds, when they're applied during the brooding season they can cause chicks to starve, because they're dependent on insects for food. To make matters worse, sage grouse are highly susceptible to West Nile virus, which was first seen in sage grouse in 2002. Evaporation ponds associated with mining and fracking serve as breeding grounds for the mosquitoes that carry the virus. Mosquito numbers were up by about 75 percent in 2006.

Gail Patricelli, a professor in the department of evolution and ecology at the University of California in Davis, is doing some interesting research with sage grouse. She's trying to see if the volume of a cock bird's call on a lek influences how female sage grouse select the male they'll mate with. A bioacoustics researcher at Cornell found that male sage grouse sound displays are highly directional and beamed laterally from the vocal sacs. This means that male birds often stand next to—rather than in front of—females who are watching the males in the lek so that their loudest sounds are coming right at the females. Who knew?

Patricelli worked with Cornell's Lab of Ornithology and its bioacoustics research program to develop a way to measure the noise level coming from any particular male bird. To get a better idea about what was happening on the lek, they built a robotic female sage grouse, which held a number of microphones and video cameras that recorded not only the sounds but also the movements of the male birds. And because females move around the strutting area, the robotic grouse was outfitted with wheels that ran on a little railroad-like track so it could move back and forth in a mechanical approximation of a live female bird. By understanding sexual selection and how sage grouse might adapt their vocalizations and movements for maximum effect, Patricelli hopes to provide insight into exactly how sensitive these birds are to other noises in their environment.

Patricelli and several graduate students are conducting a

five-year study on the effects of noise from energy development near the Pinedale area. By using the robotic grouse, researchers are honing in on sounds produced by individual sage grouse strutting on the leks. They're also isolating and characterizing the major sounds associated with energy development, such as noise from compressors, drilling rigs, and roads. To do this they use ARUs—autonomous recording units—to measure how sound travels through the environment over short (fewer than fifty meters) and long (one to five kilometers) distances and over a variety of ground types, vegetation types, and terrains. These ARUs are remote recorders that place sounds directly onto a hard drive at preset times throughout the day. The sounds are then analyzed with pattern-recognition software in a lab.

Once they figure out what noises are in the area and where they're coming from, Patricelli's group will conduct a series of experiments to see how the grouse respond to controlled noise placed at different distances from their leks. Ultimately, they hope to develop a model that will allow energy companies and land managers to predict how different sounds at given locations will affect grouse breeding behaviors.

Why should someone like Steve care about all this? It doesn't take a rocket scientist or even a biologist to tell you that at some level the noise from drilling rigs and huge trucks and seismic thumpers and compressor pumps is going to be bothersome to the sage grouse. The questions are, how much is too much, and can any of this be mitigated? Or will this kind of acoustic disturbance spell the end of any kind of lek activity near areas where natural gas or oil or coal-bed methane is being pumped out of the ground? One thing people who study sage grouse do know is that the males are extremely devoted to particular lek sites (and the females show high site fidelity to nesting and brooding sites), and no one really knows what will happen to them or where they'll go if they abandon their leks. Leks are chosen because of a very narrow set of criteria, including being open and yet in close proximity to dense sagebrush, and there's evidence that some of these leks have been active for hundreds of years. So if a lek is disturbed, where do these male birds go?

In June 2007, Audubon Wyoming produced a map showing federal mineral leases, including oil and gas, and important sage grouse habitat. In many cases, these overlap. Brian Rutledge, the executive director of Audubon Wyoming, called the map a "little terrifying" because of the implications for sage grouse and their habitat. And as goes the sage grouse, so goes the neighborhood, because sage grouse are very sensitive to change and often act as a bellwether species for the overall health of sagebrush habitat.

Probably the most important sage grouse research done recently is a study by Matt Holloran that he did as a doctoral student at the University of Wyoming in Laramie. This study was funded, in part, by EnCana Oil and Gas and the BLM. In his dissertation, Holloran found that in areas subjected to full-field natural gas development in the Pinedale Anticline and the Jonah Field, populations of breeding sage grouse males on leks decreased by an average of 51 percent from the year before development to 2004. On undisturbed leks, the decrease was 3 percent. He also found that males at three leks surrounded by natural gas development declined by 89 percent, and two of the three leks were abandoned altogether within four years after drilling began. Active drilling within 3.1 miles of a lek, increased road traffic, and an increase in well density all contributed to reducing the number of breeding males. Females also strongly avoided nesting in areas of high well density. Overall, there was a 21 percent decline in the population of nesting females in the disturbed areas as compared to undisturbed areas. And there was a 21 percent decline in sage grouse population growth in developed gas fields, which could be a reflection of birds leaving the area as well as of higher mortality rates. Holloran concluded that "current development stipulations are inadequate to maintain greater sage grouse in natural gas fields" and predicted the sage grouse populations would become extinct in the Pinedale Anticline and the Jonah Field within nineteen years if current population trends continue.

At least three petitions have been submitted to the U.S. Department of the Interior requesting that the sage grouse be listed as threatened or endangered. So far, all petitions have been denied.

Steve's feelings about the sage grouse are complicated. He has spent more than twenty years observing the species and has kept notes in his journal about where he's seen the birds and the number of birds he's seen. He's looked for them during all seasons and has found cock birds strutting and booming on leks; brooding females who sit so determinedly on their eggs that he's almost stepped on them; sage grouse families walking near pools of water in early summer; flocks of young grouse flying with the hens in early autumn; and, finally, enormous mixed flocks of hen and cock birds on their wintering grounds. Steve's taken enough footage of the birds to produce a DVD about the life history of the sage grouse. He always has a video and still camera with him, and when he has enough footage he puts everything together in his house in Salt Lake City. He calls his production company Sky King Productions and sells his DVDs through some falconry catalogs. The sage grouse DVD is his latest, and in the narration he speaks eloquently about the threats to the sage grouse in Wyoming, including natural gas exploration and habitat degradation from overgrazing.

If Steve's not talking about his falcons he's talking about sage grouse. "The biggest lek in the whole county is behind the cabin," he told me, "which means there's still a lot of grouse out there." Last year he counted 265 birds on that lek. He used to think that a big lek was more than a hundred birds, but here's one that's approaching three hundred, and those birds are strutting right behind his house. "They've been strutting there for longer than people have been studying them, and we still didn't know it existed. They've done some studies—and the studies are good—but they're generally done by students who look at an area and then move on. And here they want to have these birds listed but they still don't really know anything about them."

Steve soft-sells threats to the sage grouse because the bottom line is he thinks the grouse are doing fine. He thinks there are far too few field biologists studying the species in Wyoming for them to make judgments about the status of the population, and he resents it when I bring up the results of some study.

"Look, they do study sage grouse, but I look at these birds more than any human being in the world. I look at them every day, and I have never once encountered a biologist in the field," he said. "Wait, that's not true. I was going to photograph a lek in Pinedale last year and I did see one guy out there studying the lek, but that was one guy and it was last year and I've been doing this for twenty years. I haven't seen any decline in the population in twenty years. I'm actually finding new leks and wintering areas all the time. Wyoming Game and Fish did a survey behind my house and they didn't find any leks. I went out there and found nine."

"But, Steve, what about what's going on with natural gas exploration?" I asked. "Didn't that displace some big leks in the Jonah Field?" He's so disgusted by what's happened there that he won't drive through it. One of his favorite hunting places— White Rainbow wintering grounds—was smack-dab in the middle of Jonah Field, near where the old windmill still stands. But he skirted the question and went on to say the grouse are doing fine because he still sees flocks of up to a thousand on the wintering grounds. It's all about the wintering grounds, he said, and as long as there's habitat left to support these huge flocks of birds through the winter, he thinks they'll be okay.

I asked what he'd do if they list the sage grouse.

He's always quiet when I ask that question, but lately, as it looks more like an inevitability, he's said that he'll switch to hunting jackrabbits with gyrfalcons. And he said, "I'm not worried about them being listed. I don't care about that—I just think that they should really know if they warrant listing. I don't want to see them list any species for political reasons—it should be based on the biology of the species because if they're not endangered and they put them on that list, it makes the program less credible.

"You know, you're a lot more thorough when you're finding the birds out of a love for them rather than an assignment. I have to know where the grouse are because I don't want to waste my time riding around in my truck when I've got birds to fly." And with that he turned his attention to talking about the great grouse hawking season he's going to have with his falcons Jomo and Tava and Jahanna and the new bird he's training, and he said it with a manic intensity, as if he realized it might be his last grouse hawking season ever.

15
The Falconer

ONE TIME WHEN we were talking about death, Steve said he never wanted to be a drain on his family physically or financially, so if he was getting old and needy in some way he was going to go to the wilderness to be eaten by a bear. As preparation for this, he thought he might start learning about bears and go study their habits and photograph them. When the time came, he would head out to a mountain, take a hunk of bacon with him, rub it all over himself, then lie down and wait. I said, "You know they'll kill the bear if they figure out what happened." Steve got quiet for a minute, then said he would make sure he found a really remote site so that he—and the bear—would never be found.

If you really dig into who a person is and look at what he loves and hates and then spend as much time chitchatting with him about life-and-death matters as you do the weather, he starts to take shape. People are a mass of contradictions, and Steve is certainly no exception. He's driven, intense, maniacal, strong, handsome, weathered, rugged, fast, wiry, loyal, generous, responsible, stoic, mechanical, clever, focused, gregarious, extremely hard-working, philosophical, apolitical, confident, and unsure of himself; a drinker, a hunter, a photographer, an aficionado of simple food, a storyteller, a one-eyed falconer, a loner, a father, and a husband.

At his core, he's a westerner, and that fact informs everything he does and thinks. A descendant of Mormon pioneers who helped settle Salt Lake City, a hundred and sixty years later Steve lives fewer than ten miles from the canyon where his pioneer ancestors first walked into the Great Salt Lake Basin. This actual proximity to the ancestral footpath has had a profound effect on Steve. He grew up in that canyon and came to know and love every inch of the ridges and gullies that defined his childhood. And I can't help but think that Steve's industriousness and work ethic come from those pioneers who embodied that indomitable spirit when they walked through his childhood realm and into the unknown frontier.

Early one evening, I went with Steve to watch him participate in an Eagle Court—the ceremony an Eagle Scout goes through when he's awarded that rank. It's the highest rank a Boy Scout can achieve, and only a small percentage of boys go all the way through to this level. Steve told me that Utah has the greatest number of Eagle Scouts in the country because all the Latter-day Saints churches sponsor scouting troops. Scout meetings count as church meetings, and, according to Steve, the more church meetings you have, the higher up the ladder you go. I guess that'd be the ladder to heaven.

Steve was in great demand for these Eagle Courts because he had a bald eagle he could bring to the ceremony. "I've been to more LDS churches than Brigham Young ever even dreamed of," he said. He doesn't pretend to be any different than who he is just because he's in a Mormon church—he doesn't bare his soul in testimony, which he said the Mormons do in their meetings. "I think they find what I say refreshing," he said.

Before the Eagle Court began, we sat in his truck in the church parking lot with Liberty, the male bald eagle, perched in the back. It was a hot, hot summer day but thunderheads were building over the distant lake and the wind was starting to pick up. Two young mothers with about five kids between them sat on quilts spread on the grass next to the church door, having a little picnic. The father of the Eagle Scout drove up, got out of his car, came over to Steve's window, and introduced himself. He was probably in his late thirties, wearing a dark suit that might have fit him a decade earlier; the years of good eating showed. As he shook Steve's hand he wiped his forehead with a handkerchief. He seemed nervous, and he said as much. Steve told him to relax and that he was sure it would be a lovely ceremony. The man went into the church to help set up chairs while we continued waiting in the truck.

The air was getting thick and heavy with the anticipation of rain. The wind began to whip the American flag that flew on a pole near the front door. The women packed up their picnic baskets and stood and grabbed the edges of the quilts and attempted to fold them while gusts of wind tried to tear them from their hands.

I guess sitting in a church parking lot got Steve thinking, and while we waited he launched into his view of religion. He said people want to make everything into a nice neat story and that he thought they just went with the flow because it was easy and because that's how their parents did it. Pretty soon, he said, the religion defined who they were.

"How can everybody accept that one being created everything on this planet? It makes Santa Claus coming down every chimney seem like nothing," he said. "If someone really wanted to get into it with me about God creating everything, I'd say I think God must look like an insect. Why would he make so many beetles and so few primates? Maybe his beetles are his obsession like falconry is mine."

Steve said that instead of saying *one nation, under God* in the Pledge of Allegiance, he quietly substitutes *one nation, under the sun*. He thinks we should worship the sun because once it burns out, there won't be anything else here. And when he looks at the stars at night, he thinks about infinity—there's no end to outer space—and then wonders how it can be that way. "I think infinity is hard for humans to grasp. If the universe is infinite then the odds of two people who look exactly the same as you and me and sitting in the same colored car sitting somewhere else out there are infinite. The places that are like Earth out there are more numerous than there are grains of sand on this planet. It can be exactly the same somewhere else," he said. "That's a hard thing for us to grasp, but I think it's cool."

The big wind soon brought huge splattering raindrops onto the windshield of the truck and then a deluge. The inside of the windshield fogged up as we talked about infinity and whether or not there was a God and what some different religions were like. He told me that Julie was raised in some religion but he didn't know what that religion was because she hadn't gone to church since he'd met her. "Isn't that amazing? We've been married for over twenty years and I don't know that about her," he said.

The rain let up and the nervous father motioned us into the church. Steve got Liberty from the back of the truck and carried the eagle on his gloved fist into the entryway. When it was time, he carried Liberty past the punch bowl and down the center aisle, between the rows of metal folding chairs that held the Eagle Scout's friends and family.

Steve stood at the front of the room and talked about the anthropomorphized virtues of an eagle—virtues like paying attention to one's family and being brave in the face of danger. He looked right at the Eagle Scout as he spoke and told him that by achieving this rank, he had proven he had these same attributes. The eagle glared. The parents got weepy. I stood in the back by the punch bowl and looked at the little shrine to the Eagle Scout that had been arranged on the table. It was a tableau of school pictures and photographs of his Eagle Scout community project and a letter of congratulations from a local politician. And I thought about how this young man probably didn't think too much about infinity and the presence of God and the effects on the universe if the sun burned out tomorrow. So far his world was most likely defined and limited by the people sitting in this room.

Later that night I tried to figure out what the conversation in the truck had been all about and decided it was just part of the paradox of who Steve is. Here's a man who exudes confidence yet requires reassurance. A man who wants to be with his wife yet won't compromise by limiting the time he spends flying his birds. A man who's an extremely generous and gracious host yet whines that people take advantage of him and his cabin. A man who wants his employees to take on more responsibility yet won't delegate tasks to them because he believes no one can do the job as well as he can. A man who creates the fiercest falcons on the planet yet gambles with their lives by flying them when eagles are around.

Tim reminded me that other falconers don't see Steve the way I see him. They don't see his complicated nature; they see a tough, intense, unyielding falconer who's periodically over the top. "What's interesting is that if you get to know him, you realize he's dead serious in everything he does," said Tim. "He doesn't really have a sense of irony. He has no perspective on himself unless it's for a set piece in one of his stories and that's just the showman kicking in."

"I remember seeing him at a falconry meet in the seventies," one falconer said. "We were flying birds over a nice duck pond that had a thin layer of ice on part of it, and we didn't have any dogs to flush the ducks that were at the far end of the pond. Never wanting to let a good hunting opportunity go to waste, Steve took off his coat and the next thing I knew he's doing a swan dive into the icy water."

Another time he was flying his bird in Malad, Idaho, during the winter when his bird caught a duck and ended up on the opposite side of a half-frozen river. Steve knew that once that bird had eaten its fill of the duck he'd have trouble getting it to come back, so he took off all of his clothes, threw his hunting bag and glove across the river to the opposite bank, then took a running leap and jumped toward the crumbling remains of a washed-out bridge. He somehow managed to grab hold of some pieces of rebar attached to a stone abutment and swung himself over to the shore. He grabbed his bag and glove and sprinted across the frozen ground to his bird, which was feeding on the duck. After slipping his glove on, he took the falcon off the duck and put the carcass in the hawking bag. He then ran back to the river, took the duck out of the bag, showed it to his bird, and flung the carcass across the river. The falcon flew right to the duck, landed on it, and continued plucking feathers from its still warm breast. Then Steve threw the hawking bag and glove back across the river. Unfortunately, there was no rebar to catch on the way back, so Steve plunged into the icy water and swam, dodging chunks of ice floating past. As all this was happening a small plane appeared overhead and buzzed the area several times—probably trying to figure out what the heck was going on with the naked man in the frozen river.

Steve has spent nights on mountains searching for lost birds, and one time he spent twenty-four hours in the desert with no water while he was looking for a lost falcon. He's hired planes to take him above lost birds to try to track telemetry signals. He takes his responsibility to his falcons completely to heart, and the lengths he will go to to retrieve a bird rivals the efforts of parents searching for lost children.

I think this combination of earnestness and intensity is what's great about Steve. Most hard-core falconers have been greatly influenced by Frederick II's thirteenth-century book *The Art of Falconry*. Translated into English in 1943, it shows up on the bookshelves of serious falconers around the world. But few have taken Frederick's words to heart the way Steve has. As we were driving back from the Eagle Court ceremony, Steve told me he'd started the only King Frederick Celebration he knew of. For about a decade, a score of Utah falconers would gather for a weekend in October to fly their birds and hold the King Frederick Celebration. They'd read aloud the section in Frederick's book about the falconer's qualifications before doing the archery competition and the falconer's dash. "Most years there'd be about a dozen falconers participating," said Steve. "Mainly young guys in good shape."

It takes nothing for me to imagine Steve standing in front of a group of men, holding this huge volume in his hands, reading the falconer's qualifications according to Frederick in his sonorous voice and believing every single word. He'd read:

> The falconer should be of medium size; if he is too tall he is likely to be easily tired and not nimble; on the other hand, if he is too small his movements, either on horseback or on foot, may be too quick and too sudden. He ought to be moderately fleshy, so that he is not handicapped by emaciation and thus be unable to do hard work or to withstand the cold, nor should he be so fat that he is likely to shun exertion and suffer from the heat. The falconer must not be one who belittles his art and dislikes the labor involved in his calling. He must be diligent and persevering, so much so that as old age approaches he will still pursue the sport out of pure love of it. For, as the cultivation of an art is long and new methods are constantly introduced, a man should never desist in his efforts but persist in its practice while he lives, so that he may bring the art itself nearer to perfection. He must possess marked sagacity; for, though he may, through the teachings of experts, become familiar with all the requirements involved in the whole art of falconry, he will still have to use all his natural ingenuity in devising means of meeting emergencies. Indeed, one cannot easily set down in writing all the special duties and contingencies that may arise in consequence of either the good or the bad behavior of birds

of prey. Since the habits of birds vary greatly, the falconer must be resourceful in applying whatever he has gleaned from this book.

The falconer should also possess a retentive memory, that he may keep in mind both the good and the evil that he encounters in his contacts with falcons, whether they be his own, the bird's, or of some other origin; he must cultivate the good and avoid the bad.

He should also have good eyesight and see well in the distance, so that he can keep in view—very necessary, this— the birds at which he wishes to fly his hawk; also his own falcon must not be lost to view when she is at a distance. He ought, in addition, to keep a sharp lookout on everything in the locality where he is hunting.

It goes without saying that the falconer's hearing should be acute, so that he can readily hear and identify the call notes of birds he is looking for, especially in the presence of other avian sounds. He must also be able to recognize the voices of his associates and the tones of the bells on his own hawk (that may have flown out of sight), and may even from the call of birds discover the direction of his falcon's flight.

A falconer should have a good carrying voice so that his falcons can hear his signals when they are far apart; and his assistants will be able to understand his directions more easily if he has a strong voice. He must be alert and agile in his movements, that there may be no delay in assisting his falcons when the necessity arises.

He must be of a daring spirit and not fear to cross rough and broken ground when this is needful. He should be able to swim in order to cross unfordable water and follow his bird when she has flown over and requires assistance.

He should not be too young, as his youth may tempt him to break the rules governing his art. Young people tend to become bored and to be attracted only by successful and pleasing flights. Still, we do not include all youths in this category, since some of them become good carriers of falcons. But, speaking generally, they are not adapted to the tasks required in the taming and the training of birds for the chase; nor should they be allowed at first to fly the falcons. They ought to wait until they not only are skilled in the art but have reached manhood's estate.

The falconer must not be a sleepyhead, nor a heavy sleeper, for much is required of him—he goest to bed late, he must make several necessary inspections of the birds at nighttime, and he must rise early, often before daylight. The falconer ought to be a light sleeper, also, to enable him to hear the falcon's bells, the flapping of the bird's wings, or other indications of her unrest.

He should not be the slave of his stomach (neither too voracious, nor an epicure), whether at home or in the open country; because, if perchance he has lost his hunting falcon, such a one would rather turn back to seek a meal before he has found her or, if at home, he may neglect his bird, forgetting her in the indulgence of his gluttony.

A drunkard is useless. Inebriety is one of those minor forms of insanity that soon ends in destroying the usefulness of a bird; because, although the inebriated attendant may believe he is treating her well, neither he nor any other simpleton should be allowed to have the care of a falcon.

A bad temper is a grave failing. A falcon may frequently commit acts that provoke the anger of her keeper, and unless he has his temper strictly under control he may indulge in improper acts toward a sensitive bird so that she will very soon be ruined.

Laziness and neglect in an art that requires so much work and attention are absolutely prohibited.

The falconer must not be an absent-minded wanderer, lest because of his erratic behavior he fail to inspect his falcons as often as he should. A hawk may be seriously damaged in a short time, and therefore requires frequent inspection.

As he reads those words Steve knows in his heart that according to Frederick, he is a true falconer. He is connected by a thin thread made from the strands of passion, dedication, and experience to every obsessed falconer who ever flew a bird. And when he flies his birds above a prickly sagebrush desert in Wyoming, he knows he's not alone and that there are hard-core falconers flying birds everywhere, from the burning hot sand in Arabia to an agricultural field in China to a steep heather-covered mountain slope in Scotland. This intimate connection between man and bird spans the globe and dips back thousands of years into human history.

And Steve thinks himself the luckiest man on earth.

16

Nebraska

EVERY YEAR, during the week of Thanksgiving, falconers from all over the country come together to reconnect and brag about their birds and watch one another fly. This annual meet is sponsored by the North American Falconers' Association and is usually held somewhere in the middle of the country, in a spot where there's lots of open agricultural land, ponds, and hedgerows—prime areas for game and hunting with birds. NAFA finds a local hotel that's receptive to hunters and hunting dogs and birds and then reserves a huge block of rooms. Recently, the NAFA meet was held in Kearney, Nebraska, and Tim and I decided to leave our family behind—not an easy decision when you have kids and it's Thanksgiving and someone has to take care of all the animals—and fly to Nebraska to hang out with the falconers.

The two-hour drive from the airport in Lincoln to Kearney was across an unremarkable section of Nebraska. Some part of me expected to see the tall grass of virgin prairie waving in the breeze, although I knew that couldn't possibly be the case. Nonetheless, pioneer accounts of the area ran through my head as we traveled across the state. Of course it's all agricultural lands now—lots of corn and soybeans and pastureland and shelterbelts. The fields weren't as huge as those you might see in Kansas, and the topography wasn't nearly as flat. There were actually areas around Kearney with undulating hills and little gullies and creeks and ponds. Sometimes we'd see an area of pastureland that didn't look gnawed down to the ground, and we could tell there were some native grasses still growing there. At one point, off a side road, we passed a small prairie dog town—holes with piles of dirt near them and prairie dogs sitting up on their haunches near the holes. We stopped the car and heard them whistling and saw them diving for the cover of their holes. They are so curious that within a minute they were popping back out and scampering across the grass in search of God-knows-what.

Tim and I drove over the Platte River just south of Kearney, then drove about ten miles to pay a visit to Fort Kearny (Fort Kearny has no *e* in it because it was named after General Stephen Kearny—I can't explain the existence of the second *e* in the town's name). Fort Kearny was an important fort on the Oregon and Mormon trails because it was the first one the settlers came to as they followed the Platte River on their way west. It was built in 1848 to protect the pioneers from the Indians, and in its twenty-three years as a military outpost, it was never attacked by Indians. The fort was located just north of a settlement that was called Dobytown, because the hovels in it were made from adobe. Dobytown was also an important stop on the Oregon Trail since it had prostitutes and liquor and outrageously expensive goods for sale.

Where the main part of the fort once stood was now a cornfield. Tim and I wandered along the edge of the parkland and read the placards that showed what buildings should have been standing in front of us. Instead of buildings, though, we were looking at row after row of corn stubble. After an archaeological survey in the last half of the twentieth century, foot-high wooden posts were placed along what would have been the perimeters of long-gone buildings such as the men's quarters and the warehouse. At one end of the park someone had built a replica stockade on a raised berm. Inside, along the wall, was a long sign with facsimiles of telegrams sent from the fort to Washington begging for reinforcements because army scouts had seen Sioux and Pawnee gathering by the river. Although the soldiers at the fort never actually fought the Indians, the mere fact that the Indians were out there made them nervous. Fort Kearny was also home to a Pony Express stop.

I thought about Steve's ancestors; they must have traveled past this very spot when they pulled their belongings west as part of the great Mormon handcart migration. I wondered if Steve was as drawn to the Mormon Trail as I was—if he felt compelled to stand in the ruts created by all those handcarts and wagons a hundred and fifty years ago.

As it happened, the International Association for Falconry was holding its annual general meeting in conjunction with the NAFA meet—something that had never occurred before. Because of that, the Peregrine Fund had invited a group of falconers to come a day early to travel to Boise, Idaho, to visit the Archives of Falconry, which is an independent arm of the Peregrine Fund's World Center for Birds of Prey. Early in the morning, before catching the bus to the little airport where we'd get a chartered flight to Boise, we had been delighted to see that some of the falconers from other countries were wearing their native dress. It was neat to look around and see the Czech falconer decked out in a loden green boiled-wool jacket, the Kazakh falconers in pantaloons and bright jackets and tall hats, and the young Japanese man, who looked more like a samurai warrior than a falconer, with his long hair tied in a bun on his head and wearing flowing clothes. About a hundred and fifty of us loaded into four buses in front of the Holiday Inn early that morning, which got us to the airport on the outskirts of Kearney. Once there, we boarded a 737 charter jet that the Emirates Falconers Club had paid for; its members wanted us to see the new Arabian falconry wing—the Sheikh Zayed Arab Falconry

Heritage Wing—that had just been built onto the archives and library building. At least one American falconer declined the invitation because of the Arabian connection, a kind of misplaced post-9/11 anti-Taliban protest.

The Peregrine Fund's buildings occupy the top of a hill, where the organization owns five hundred acres. The view from the hilltop is breathtaking, with the city of Boise and the Rocky Mountains off in the distance. The compound includes offices, a small visitors' center, the archives and museum, and a number of barns where birds are housed for the captive-breeding projects. One thing the Peregrine Fund does is boost the numbers of extremely rare raptors—such as California condors—through captive breeding and carefully managed release programs.

The inside walls of the archives and library building hold beautiful paintings and lithographs of falcons and falconers and European and American hunting scenes. Majestic white gyrfalcons perch on lichen-covered cliffs in the Arctic. Peregrines stoop and pursue red grouse in a Scottish moor in an artistic display of power. Dainty merlins ride hooded on the fists of Victorian-era-clad ladies traveling sidesaddle. The archives house some great artifacts, including Colonel Thomas Thornton's Georgian silver-gilt tea urn (presented to him by the Confederate Hawks of Great Britain and one of the most important and lovely artifacts in British falconry history) and Colonel Thornton's muzzle-loading shotgun (1801). Thornton was a larger-than-life eighteenth-century sportsman and falconer whose exploits in the field were chronicled in books and prints.

In one large case near Colonel Thornton's silver urn there's a first-rate collection of leather hoods ranging in size from tiny ones that would fit a kestrel up to hoods large enough to fit the head of a bald eagle. The library is slowly amassing an extensive collection of falconry ephemera, and the archivists just finished cataloging several boxes of documents related to Operation Falcon. This will be helpful to those interested in trying to sort out what happened in the early 1980s, when the American falconry community went through its own version of a McCarthy-like era, complete with spies and undercover agents and sting operations.

The finishing touches were being put on the new Arab wing, and the paint was drying on some of the signs that had just been finished that morning in preparation for our visit. The centerpiece of the new wing was a beautiful, large camelhair hunting tent filled with all the accoutrements of Middle Eastern falconry, including a gorgeous Oriental carpet, Arabian falconry equipment and furniture (including perches and hoods), and an Arabian coffee service. A couple of mannequins dressed in flowing Arab robes rounded out the display. Video monitors showed films of Arabian falconers holding beautiful birds and desert scenes of gyrfalcons flying on houbara bustards.

It was interesting to be around so many falconers, because it turns out they're so much alike. They're intense and focused, and it became clear that the passion for falconry runs deep. *Once a falconer, always a falconer* cycled through my thoughts as I watched men—who were long past the stage when they should be running—run through fields to help their birds hunt. One reason I wanted to go to the NAFA meet was to see other falconers and watch them in action. I wondered if hanging out with Tim and Steve was giving me a skewed impression of what falconry was all about. I wanted to see how falconers behaved in their own community, with their own kind. I felt a little like Margaret Mead on an anthropological quest to unravel the mysteries of a culture. And, like Mead, I had to learn the language and figure out how to interpret cultural and social cues. Unlike Mead, though, I was immersed in a community that was nothing like Samoa; the most exotic location I found myself in over the course of the meet was a feedlot. But it was a strange, foreign world of testosterone and adrenaline and, at times, passionate pursuit as falconers attempted to locate game for their birds to fly at.

I can't imagine what other guests at the Holiday Inn in Kearney must have thought when they passed guys walking through the halls of the hotel with huge birds of prey on their fists or when they saw the weathering yard, where a fine assortment of birds were perched out, getting some air. And there was the extra freezer that stood near a door to the parking lot; as the meet progressed, it began to fill with game caught by the birds—ducks and squirrels and rabbits and a prairie chicken or two.

The weathering yard, marked by a temporary snow fence, covered a large section of lawn behind the hotel. People hung around the fence looking at the goshawks and red-tails and Barbary falcons and gyrfalcons and peregrines and gyr-peregrine hybrids and, of course, Harris's hawks and a couple of Cooper's hawks and merlins. The birds were tied to perches stuck into the ground and spaced about every five feet. Each bird had enough room to hop into the plastic bath pan that was filled with water and set right next to its perch, but not enough length on its leash to reach the neighboring bird. The bath pans were round or rectangular and all different sizes depending on the bird. A bird like a peregrine might hop down into the bath pan and get almost completely submerged and ruffle its feathers and shake and flop around a bit, then return to the perch and face the sun and spread its wings to dry.

The parking lot was filled with trucks—many of them four-wheel drive—with enclosed beds to hold kennels for the dogs and perches for the birds. Some falconers had devised ingenious ways of attaching the perches to the inside of the truck. Steve just has two-by-eights covered with AstroTurf fastened to a heavy piece of metal that sits in his truck bed. Shawn Hayes, a falconer from California, has his perches rigged so the AstroTurf-covered wooden perch slides out on rails, and he doesn't have to reach into the truck to secure his birds—he just slides the perch out, secures the bird, then slides it back. Falconers milled around the parking lot wearing camouflage-pattern clothing and overalls with leather chaps sewn onto them in parts where they'd wear thin quickly. It was a chance to show off falconry T-shirts advertising previous NAFA and California Hawking Club meets and sky trials. Sky trials are also known as pigeon derbies: falcons are sent to soar in the sky, and then really fast homing pigeons are thrown up for them to chase. The falcon's performance is rated by how high it goes and whether it gets close to or hits a pigeon in a stoop.

There was a lot of standing around in the parking lot that ran between the weathering yard and in the hotel hallways, waiting for something to happen. Clumps of falconers and falconer wannabes their badges hanging from lanyards around their necks identifying them by name and state or country—talked to one another and admired birds that were perched out or were being put into the backs of trucks. A kind of subtle jockeying for position occurred the whole time. It's important for a falconer to keep an eye roaming around the crowd, looking for the best falconer flying the kind of bird he wants to see fly. He waits for that falconer to pick up his bird from the yard, hood it, and then walk toward his truck. Once he's opened the back of his truck and is getting ready to tether the bird to the perch, the first falconer can walk over and casually ask the guy if he minds if someone watches him fly his bird.

There's a real hierarchy of falconers, and some of the falconers at that meet held a kind of mythical status. There was Steve, and Dave Cherry, and Shawn Hayes, and Tony Huston (some of his fame comes from the fact that his father is John, his grandfather is Walter, and his sister is Angelica), and those falconers walked around with a kind of bubble surrounding them—they knew they were hot stuff and they knew that everyone wanted to see them fly their birds. Then the caravans of vehicles started to form as people pulled their cars and trucks into a line behind the falconer's truck.

Some of the NAFA people had come to Kearney a week or so early to scout around for good flying spots. They drove through the countryside looking for congregations of prairie chickens or pheasants or ducks or rabbits and then asked the landowners for permission to fly on the land. Most landowners said yes right away because they were really curious about the sport and wanted to see it all unfold. Others had to be convinced.

Robert Bagley and Shawn Hayes came to the meet early to scout locations for longwingers and took a small plane up to look for good duck ponds. Shawn sat in the back seat with binoculars, and as the plane was being buffeted by winds, he tried to glass the ponds for ducks. He finally had to give up because the jiggling got magnified when he looked through binoculars, and it was making him feel sick. Bagley took the GPS coordinates of the best-looking ponds and marked them onto maps. His next job was to locate and visit the landowners. One guy he visited was the manager of Fort Kearny Consolidated, a huge feedlot operation filled with cows and steers in various states of readiness for market. There were three little ponds covered with ducks behind the feedlots in some back pastures. At first the manager said, "No way, we don't allow hunting on the property." Then Bagley tried a different tack and talked about flying falcons as a form of exercising the bird and said that the falcon might or might not catch a duck. "Isn't that hunting?" asked the manager. Finally, Bagley convinced the guy to let the falconers fly their birds over the ponds on the condition that they didn't spook the cows. Seemed reasonable until we got there; we were sneaking through the field, and a herd of about thirty young and curious red and black Angus cattle walked toward us to investigate. When Shawn Hayes took some steps toward them, they hauled ass out of there. It showed me how easily a stampede could get started.

Something became really apparent at the NAFA meet: this sport is decidedly male and definitely graying. You could count the number of women falconers on one hand, and most of the falconers at the meet ranged in age from fifty to about ninety. There were a number of overweight men flying birds (mostly the buteos), and it didn't look as if they'd have an easy time crashing through the woods kicking up bunnies or chasing down squirrels. More than one falconer reminded me of Edmund Gwenn, the actor who played Kris Kringle in *Miracle on Thirty-fourth Street*. These older men had begun flying birds before the federal government enacted laws regulating falconry. They'd gotten their first birds when they were teenagers and had been flying falcons or hawks ever since. Some of the early "made" birds (hybrids) were at the meet and, like their owners, were still going strong. These twenty-year-old birds, like Jomo, would certainly have been dead by this time if they were in the wild. (Wait a minute—they wouldn't even have existed in the wild.) These older falconers really are the connective tissue to the previous generation of great falconers who were flying birds in the 1930s, '40s, and '50s—legendary falconers such as Frank Beebe, Hal Webster, Al Nye, Cornelius McFadden, and the Craighead brothers.

Tim and I scored a spot in a caravan the first afternoon. Kearney was experiencing the weirdest weather—the whole week was predicted to be twenty degrees above normal for that time of year—and this kind of warmth was not good for gyrfalcons or even gyr-peregrine hybrids. A gyrfalcon is a bird from the Arctic. It spends its life hunting the tundra or around ice and snow. What the heck would it do with seventy-degree days with no moisture? When it's that warm, they expend a lot of energy just panting, trying to cool down. They also fly sluggishly, which isn't surprising. We ended up riding in a van with a falconer from Massachusetts and his wife; Peter Devers, a falconer from Millbrook, New York; and Andrew, a falconer from Britain who was working for Nick Fox, a legendary British falconer, in his bird breeding project in Wales. Andrew had recently published a book about falconry in British literature, a version of his dissertation. When I asked him if he'd read any twentieth-century texts, he gave me a look and said he'd stopped at the end of the seventeenth century. Okay.

About forty of us went by caravan and ended up in a farmer's field. The farmer came out to watch the flights. Lots of the international falconers were there—the Japanese, the Belgians, the French, and the South Americans—so the pressure was on for the Americans to perform well. NAFA was intent on showing the foreign falconers how American falconry worked. The longwingers were desperate to fly on prairie chickens. Much smaller prey than sage grouse, a prairie chicken weighs two and a half pounds at most, but these birds are in the grouse family and are very good flyers. They're nonmigratory birds that hang out in social groups. Tony Huston got out his gyr-peregrine cross, Johnnie, a beautiful white bird, and after doing some scouting around for birds on foot, he decided to put him up. I'd seen this bird fly in Wyoming and he did love to land on things, and, with it being so warm, he was—like all of us—acting a bit sluggish. The prairie chickens flushed when Johnnie was out of position and ended up flying down into a draw with Johnnie in pursuit. Out came the telemetry receiver and off went Tony to walk the draw, listening for the beeps of the transmitter attached to his bird's tail. We all deserted Tony and headed off in search of more flights.

Somehow, our van made a wrong turn and we ended up pulling into an electrical power substation because we saw a bunch of falconer vehicles there. As soon as we got out of the van I said to Peter, "Those don't look like longwingers." I looked at the three young women with tattered jeans and T-shirts and exotically dyed hair sitting cross-legged on the ground, and, sure enough, a burly-looking Australian fellow emerged from fussing around in the back of a truck, and he was holding a huge Finnish goshawk—a striking bird with lovely gray feathers outlined in black and a fierce look. But this bird hunts rabbits, and it was clear that the falconer intended to hunt in the brushy draw in front of the girls. He had a couple of Jack Russell/beagle–mix dogs straining on leads in front of him, just raring to dive into the brush to flush the bunnies. Good hunting, but not really what anyone in our van had had in mind.

We jumped back in the van and, thanks to cell phones, were able to track down the hunting party we'd thought we'd been following in the first place. It was late afternoon and the sun was sinking in the sky, and the dust in the air was making a brilliant pink and orange sunset. We parked by some cars on the side of a gravel road and began hiking up through a chopped cornfield to the crest of the hill, where we could see a group of falconers standing about a mile off. Along the way we passed a small pond tucked in the shelterbelt trees and saw a single hen mallard swimming around. Just then we saw a peregrine fly over the pond, pinning the duck down (there was no way that duck was going to leave the safety of the water with a killer bird overhead), and then the falcon flew back to the ridge. The entire flight was over by the time we got near the ridge, but the falconer had another peregrine to fly and was going to try it on the duck. That meant a couple of the maniac Japanese falconers were going to have to flush the duck from the pond when the falcon was high and in position over the water (they had offered to do it). When his bird was ready, the falconer gave the signal, and two guys ran at the pond, waving their arms. The duck lifted off the water, and just then the falcon folded into a stoop and headed for the duck. The duck didn't like the looks of that, and, deciding she'd rather take her chances with the weird people shouting on the edge of the pond than with the scary predator in the sky, she put into the water again. The Japanese men tried to force the duck from the pond a couple more times, but she would have none of it. Finally, the falconer threw a pheasant he had been carrying in his game bag. The pheasant flew toward the nearest trees, and the falcon put in a halfhearted chase after it, then returned to the falconer.

The day of hunting was done. The sky was now a deep shade of blue with dark orange and red along the western horizon; above the ridge in the east, the sky was filled with what looked like swaths of pink cotton batting. An old wooden windmill—that iconic symbol of the Midwest Dust Bowl era—was the only visible structure on that high eastern horizon, and as we walked through the corn stubble back toward the vehicles, I wondered if that windmill still worked and, if it did, what or who it was drawing water for. Or if it was drawing water at all, in this dry year of abnormally warm weather.

Some friends of Tim's, Will and Maria Robinson, from Douglas, Wyoming, came to visit us at the NAFA meet, and I ended up spending the day with them. Tim had stayed at their place the previous year when Will invited him to give a talk at Casper College about the rediscovery of the ivory-billed woodpecker. They have a great place on the banks of the North Platte River. Maria is a real horse-and-dog woman and has three mustangs she bought from the BLM that she trained using the round-pen method. The Robinsons have several hundred acres of land, and a pair of red-tailed hawks and a bald eagle pair nest near the river in back of their house. At that moment their place was overrun with jackrabbits, which had made Maria consider becoming an apprentice falconer. When they'd heard about the NAFA meet only a seven-hour drive from Douglas—which is nothing to a westerner—they'd decided to come down for a couple of days to visit and to check out the falconry.

We drove out to the field where Tony had flown his bird the night before, hoping for some falconry action, but no one was there, so we drove back to the Holiday Inn and lurked around the weathering yard. The Robinsons were amazed at the numbers and varieties of species of birds perched out. No two birds looked alike, particularly among the hybrids, because of the potential color combinations of two species. Falconers who fly longwings really like the gyr-peregrine hybrid because the gyrfalcon's characteristic stamina mixed with the peregrine's instinct to ring high into the sky and then wait on over the falconer allow them to hunt larger, stronger game. We also spent some time looking at the hunting dogs. There were different breeds of spaniels, setters, pointers, and terriers. Some of them were staked out beyond the weathering yard at the edge of a field, and they would prick up their ears and wag their tails when people approached. Seeing all these cool birds and dogs was exhilarating.

Tim had his own plans for the afternoon, so Will, Maria, and I were left to troll the parking lot on our own. I'd had my eye on a guy who was loading up a pretty white gyr-peregrine, and I asked if he was going hunting and if we could tag along. He seemed happy to be asked, so we positioned our car in the caravan. The hunting party turned out to be about a dozen people, including five falconers from Belgium who were dressed alike in moss green corduroy trousers and similarly colored sweaters with leather patches on the shoulders; they reminded me of the old army sweaters people used to be able to pick up at army-navy stores. One woman was wearing green suede or possibly leather knickers with long socks and sturdy hiking shoes. Very stylish group; made me look twice at my frumpy dark green corduroy trousers (at least I had had an intuitive sense that the color was hunting chic), L. L. Bean hiking boots, black T-shirt, and tan barn jacket.

David, the falconer we'd joined, hailed from Texas by way of Florida and had a thick southern drawl. He was as nice as could be and often gave a big toothy grin (which revealed a lack of basic dental care at some point in his life). He was accompanied by his wife, who was short and stocky and who chain-smoked as we stood on the gravel road discussing the game plan. David and some other NAFA people had discovered a little pond that was completely hidden from the road, about ten miles out of Kearney. We crawled through the strands of a barbed-wire fence and walked through a nice piece of prairie land. Maria and Will identified the grasses and flowers for me as we headed in the direction of the pond. We hung back as the falconer and a friend of his approached the crest of the small ridge we were on, crawling toward the edge on their bellies to avoid being seen by the ducks, if there were ducks, down below. We talked about the topography of the land, which was much lumpier than the flat and slightly undulating fields around Kearney and, as the cowpies indicated, was clearly being used as pastureland. David and his friend crept back and told us to be very quiet because they had seen about a half a dozen mallards on the pond and didn't want them to be spooked.

David unhooded his bird, grabbing the end of one stiff leather brace with his teeth and the other with his right hand and then pushing the hood forward over the bird's head and beak, and we stood about twenty yards away and watched in silence. Then David lifted his left arm until it was almost at a 120-degree angle from his body while the bird sat very still on his gloved left hand. The bird turned and looked at us for a few seconds, then slowly turned his head back, taking in the details of the landscape. He sat on David's fist for a good five minutes, but David didn't move a muscle the entire time. My arm was burning just looking at him. Finally the bird roused, lifted his tail and crapped, which most raptors do before taking off, then spread his wings and left David's fist.

Will and Maria had binoculars, and I told them to keep them on the bird. The falcon spent several minutes circling higher and higher in the sky while David and his friend once again crept toward the edge of the little ridge. When the bird was in a good position, the two guys leaped to their feet and went barreling down the steep slope toward the pond, whooping and waving their arms on the way down. We heard the rapid wing beats of the mallards as they left the pond before we saw them. One unlucky drake mallard went in the opposite direction from the rest of the birds, and the falcon folded his wings into a stoop and hit it with such force that we heard a crack from about a hundred yards away. The duck dropped to the far shore, and the falcon was on it immediately. As the two men ran around the pond to retrieve the falcon and the dead duck, Maria and Will turned to me with their mouths open; they couldn't believe what they had just seen. For one thing, they were amazed at how quickly everything had happened, and I told them the old falconry adage: it takes a red-tailed hawker ten minutes to find a hunting spot, and then he spends four hours hunting, whereas it takes a falconer four hours to find a hunting spot, and then he hunts for ten minutes.

We got in our car and left for Kearney after congratulating David. He had returned from the pond with his bird on his fist and a bloody drake mallard in his game bag; he proudly brought out the duck and held it up by one wing to show us how pretty it was. David told us that his bird was in its twelfth flying season and took ducks pretty reliably if he supplied it with a good opportunity. Just as we reached the Holiday Inn parking lot, we saw another caravan forming, so we got in line and within minutes were heading back out of town to go to the farmer's field we had visited that morning. We hooked up with another caravan of hawkers already at the farm, so there were about forty in all.

We were there to watch Dave Cherry fly his gyr-peregrine on prairie chickens. Cherry was a falconry legend. He'd been a fixture on the Southern California falconry scene for several decades—Tim had known him when he lived there—and at that point was a complete fanatic about the sport. Dave was about six and a half feet tall and thin as a string bean, with a shock of white hair that reached almost to his shoulders. Dressed in blue jeans, work boots, a baseball cap, and a T-shirt from the California Hawking Club, Dave cut quite a figure out in the field. Because of several mishaps, including a cow who ran over and flushed the dozen or so prairie chickens that were feeding in the pasture, the entire hunting party decided to relocate to a cornfield behind the farmer's house. The farmer came out to watch Dave fly his bird and told me he thoroughly enjoyed seeing these birds fly. He'd first seen falconry four years ago when the NAFA meet had also been held in Kearney, and someone had approached him about letting falconers use his fields for hunting.

Little did we know at the time, but on the other side of town there was a similar hunting scene taking place. Shawn Hayes, a falconer who's also a premier hawker from California and happens to be one of the few black falconers in America, had just put his bird up. It was climbing high into the sky when a truck came barreling down the gravel road on the edge of the field. It stopped, and a man stepped out and yelled, "Get out of my field! You can't hunt my prairie chickens, and if you don't get that bird down right now I'm gonna shoot it out of the sky!" At which point he showed them a rifle. Several of the European and all of the Japanese falconers were with Shawn and were horrified. Apparently, this guy threatened to contact the U.S. Fish and Wildlife Service about what was going on and get them in a lot of trouble. It turned out he wasn't even the landowner but the landowner's father-in-law. He'd been drinking and for some reason just went ballistic. When I heard about this, it made me wonder what Thanksgiving dinner would be like in their household the next day.

Meanwhile, back on the other side of town, I walked next to the farmer as we approached the field where Dave Cherry planned to fly his bird. The sun was just starting to sink, and it was cooling down from the day's record high in the midseven-

ties. Dave wouldn't fly his bird until it began to cool down because he knew the weather would make it fly sluggishly. Someone had seen some prairie chickens a couple of minutes earlier,
and as soon as Dave's bird took to the air, they would be pinned
down. After Dave's bird left his fist, it circled up so high into
the sky that it became just a speck. When it was way up, the
chickens flushed and the bird came hurtling down, selected one
to hit, and slammed it with a *thwack!* The chicken dropped to
some heavy brush in a small draw in pastureland adjacent to
the cornfield we were in. The falcon flew low back and forth
over the brush but would not enter. The farmer told us that the
brush was likely to be tough going and was about thigh deep.
Dave and a very small man from France crawled through the
barbed-wire fence on the edge of the field and began running
down the slope to the draw. Suddenly they were both into the
brush, and they sprang around like terriers as they worked
their way down the draw. Up and down they went, like jerky
marionettes—the brush was clearly over the Frenchman's head
and up to Dave Cherry's shoulders. They kicked up the prairie
chicken, which flushed again, and the falcon made a lackluster
stoop as the chicken flew into more brush.

When Dave Cherry came up out of the draw he called his
bird down and wouldn't accept any praise about his bird's performance.

"Your bird flew so high."

"He should have gone a third again higher," said Dave.

"What a wonderful stoop."

"He should have tried harder to follow the chicken into the
brush," said Dave.

When we got back into the car, Will remarked on how odd
it was that the egos of the falconers seemed so wrapped up in
the performances of their birds. "For God's sake," he said. "Why
do they think they can control these birds?" That's the crux of
it, because they do think they can. Falconers know how good

their birds can be and want everyone else to know it too. A falconer feels that if his bird fails in a hunt, he himself was at fault for not providing the perfect opportunity, for underestimating the wind, for flushing the game too soon, for flushing the game too late, for not finding enough game, for not encouraging the bird to go up higher, and so on. There's an endless litany of reasons why a flight on game does not end perfectly. Sometimes a falconer can control one factor, but when you put them all together and then add the unpredictability of a bird of prey, you have the sport, and the heartbreak, of falconry. And I suspect some falconers, like Dave Cherry or Steve, both of whom are complete fanatics about the sport, have a Platonic ideal in their heads of what a perfect flight and outcome would be, and if that's not achieved they're really unhappy.

Before dawn the next day, we met falconers in the lobby of the Holiday Inn for another morning of hawking. Shawn Hayes and Robert Bagley were going to lead us to some good duck ponds. Shawn, the black falconer from California with a headful of shoulder-length braids, was also a rodeo clown (another sport that's unusual for a black man to participate in). Robert Bagley owned Marshall Radio Telemetry in Salt Lake City, the maker of some of the best falconry telemetry in the world. Jamey Eddy, a falconer from Laramie, Wyoming, was in the group as well; he and Tim had both worked at the Santa Cruz Predatory Bird Research Group, although at different times, and had been in contact with each other over the years. Jamey now worked for Western EcoSystems Technology, Inc., which did wildlife studies and assessments for private companies and the government. Like Tim, Jamey flew a tiercel peregrine. Shawn planned to fly his two gyr-peregrine hybrids. The rest of the group consisted mostly of Belgians and Germans.

We drove out to the three ponds in a back pasture behind the very large feedlot owned by Fort Kearny Consolidated. This incredibly stinky operation has acres of pens that hold steers getting fattened up on corn for the market. Guys on horseback rode through the pens. It made me think about the kind of environmental nightmare feedlots produce—where does all the waste go when the cattle are so concentrated? The pens were grouped and separated by wide cement gutters. You could smell the feedlots from miles away.

Jamey's nice tiercel peregrine flew very high and wide—in fact, so high and wide that we lost track of it. Jamey, Shawn, Tim, and a young kid who was an apprentice from St. Louis, Missouri, and who flew a red-tail, were up by the first little pond getting ready to flush the ducks. At one point, Jamey ran back and forth about twenty yards in each direction to try to get his bird's attention. The ducks flushed and put into the next pond. Jamey's bird never got a flight on the ducks because it spotted a pheasant on the ground and took after that instead. Finally, Jamey had to call his bird back.

Then Shawn put his falcon up, and when some ducks flushed, his bird put in a long diagonal stoop at them, chasing them around a small stand of trees until they landed on the third pond. This happened a few more times, and then the bird finally landed on the crossbar of a big utility pole. A wild prairie falcon sat on another section of the crossbar, and the two birds looked at each other for a couple of minutes before Shawn called his bird down.

We visited that same grouping of ponds the following day, and Joe Atkinson flew a couple of gyr-peregrines there. Joe worked with English setters—Maggie and Thistle—who were beautifully trained and stood right by him when he told them to heel. Joe put his bird up, and suddenly a prairie falcon came at his bird and they tussled in the air for several minutes. This was probably the prairie falcon we'd seen the day before, but it hadn't bothered the birds then. The dogs waited at the edge of the pond while the bird got in place above Joe, and they flushed the ducks on his command. A flock of at least fifty ducks lifted from the pond and wheeled around a couple of times. They were so beautiful as they stayed together and flew about thirty feet above our heads. I could hear a whooshing sound from so many wings beating and felt a slight wing-generated wind hit my face. Soon, Joe's bird landed in a tree. We realized why when a great horned owl came out of the trees and flew low, gliding across the third pond, where many of the ducks had landed. A great horned owl can easily kill a falcon if he can catch it, so falcons are very wary and cautious when they know an owl is around. We also saw a northern harrier fly low across a neighboring field, hunting for mammals. Its bright white rump patch flashed us as it turned to head in another direction.

Later that day we had a Thanksgiving lunch at the Holiday Inn. The hotel had reservations for over a thousand, and we watched as a steady stream of nicely dressed people got out of their cars and made their way into the hotel to eat their family dinner. It seemed strange to me, because this was not our family tradition. If we had been home we'd have been sitting in a room full of family, and after dinner the crowd would thin out and about five or six of us would sit at the table with a big bottle of wine and proceed to deconstruct politics, family, happenings in the little village, and whatever other topics until the bottle was gone. The international falconers were amazed by the variety and quantity of food available: turkey, dressing, mashed potatoes, sweet potatoes with marshmallows, salads, fruit, green bean casserole, roast beef, all kinds of pies and cakes, and make-your-own sundaes.

Although I saw Steve in passing during the NAFA meet, I didn't talk to him much. Whenever I saw him, he was with international falconers—several had been at his cabin in Wyoming prior to the meet and several would be visiting after—and I could tell he was doing a great job of hosting them and showing them an intense falconry experience. It was interesting to watch him from a distance as he interacted with others. He's very polite and accommodating, which at times seems very much at odds with the stories about him I've heard from falconers who have known him for a long time.

During one of the evening programs on North American falconry, Steve gave a wonderful twenty-minute presentation on the life history of the sage grouse. His camera work and editing were really good, and the images were stunning. He narrated the entire thing without a script and kept the falconers in the room completely engaged. He really is a good showman, and his program was far superior to the other programs that evening, most of which consisted of some pretty bad PowerPoint slide shows of hawks and falcons hunting rabbits, squirrels, grouse, and pheasant.

One morning Tim and I had breakfast with Jamey Eddy, Shawn Hayes, and Joe Atkinson. Atkinson was a falconer from the Sacramento area and was in the process of moving to eastern Oregon, about sixty miles from Boise. He was building a guest mews there to accommodate the falcons of visiting falconers. He must have had some money—Jamey said it was family money made in cattle ranching—because it sounded as if he was moving to a wonderful place. Atkinson had been flying birds for years. When we saw him out in the field, he had two gyrperegrines and a golden eagle in the back of his truck. He held one of only two falconry licenses for eagles in the state of California and had worked for years with a veterinarian to help rehabilitate injured eagles. Many had wind-power injuries from the huge windmills at Altamont.

Over the years Steve had acquired a reputation for his intensity and for being completely single-minded and focused when it comes to falconry. Stories about him and his birds were legion, so much so that when you mentioned his name in a group of falconers, the Steve stories just poured out.

The talk soon turned to Steve and how outrageous he could be. Joe said that years ago he'd wanted to meet Steve Chindgren because he'd heard he was the man to meet if you wanted to fly at sage grouse. So he'd decided to buy a gyrfalcon from him. He went to Steve's home in Salt Lake City to pick up his gyr and then planned to go flying with Steve in Wyoming. Julie asked him if he'd heard of Steve's reputation, and Joe assured her he had. But he was nonetheless unprepared for what he experienced with Steve. He went on to describe a number of incidents in which Steve exhibited his prodigious temper out in the field.

There were numerous stories of fits of rage, crazy driving, and total maniacal behavior out in the field. Shawn Hayes was riding with Steve once and ordered him to pull over and let him out if he was going to drive that fast. Joe, who was a big guy, over six feet and built like a bear, had told Steve that he wasn't going to put up with his fits and to cut it out, and Steve had told him no one had ever said that to him before. Back during the Scamp days, Steve had invited Joe to visit and go flying with him. Joe couldn't believe the grouse camp setup with the Scamp, and when Steve offered him a tent with heaters set up next to the Scamp, Joe said no way, he was going to stay in the motel.

Joe had been with Steve when Steve's bird Rocky was killed. Apparently it was about ten in the morning, and they had been seeing golden eagles everywhere, but Steve had put out a dog, which went on point about thirty yards away, and Steve couldn't stand it. He'd put Rocky up, the birds flushed, and Rocky went off on a tail chase. When they'd located him three hours later, all that was left was the transmitter and a pile of feathers.

(Later, when we were talking about birds, Steve told me the Rocky story, but in his version, he'd flown Rocky so late in the day because he had been a good host and let Joe fly his birds early. "I would never fly my birds that late, but because I was being nice in letting Joe fly earlier, I was stuck," said Steve. I could see he felt awful about what had happened to Rocky, even in the retelling. "Rocky was a great bird," he said.)

I myself had seen Steve do things that he knew were wrong, primarily because an opportunity had presented itself—like run Tucker on a bad leg because Steve was so intent on getting a good point and didn't want to rely on Earl, who was trustworthy but slower out in the field. It was as if he couldn't help himself. Still, I said I thought he had mellowed, and they agreed that he had.

It was hard for me to hear the stories about Steve. I knew they were spilling out of these guys because they were on a roll and were engaged in a kind of one-upmanship. The point was that everyone had "outrageous Steve" stories. But I knew that there wasn't a falconer at that table who didn't admire Steve's amazing hawking and training skills. Still, as the falconers talked, I found myself feeling defensive and wanting to speak up for a man who had become a good friend over the previous year and whom I knew as a kind and generous host. I wanted to say, *You don't understand him.* But I didn't interrupt to protest, because I had seen some of this behavior in Steve myself. So I sat quietly and listened, and I felt my face flush from a deep sense of my own betrayal. I felt like a coward.

17

Death in the Sage

ONE DAY ON THE PHONE Steve told me what falconry meant to him. "Falconry is defined as hunting wild quarry with a trained raptor. But for some people the hardest part about falconry is actually doing it," he said. "People who live in an area where they can't provide quarry can go out in a field and provide a hot-air balloon that they'll train their birds to fly up to. A piece of meat is attached to a small hot-air balloon and a bird is sent up after it. That makes it really easy, because they don't have to find game. And it becomes quite a little social thing where they all meet together and they all use the same balloon and they put it up there and have some beers and enjoy watching the powerful flight of the falcon. I enjoy watching them fly too—I definitely enjoy seeing them fly—but falconry's really about the hunt."

I periodically came back to the words of Steve's friend Gary Boberg, about how Steve didn't feel right if he hadn't killed something that day. When he'd said it, I'd been a little horrified by the statement and chalked it up to a bit of hyperbole, but the more I watched Steve hunt, the more I understood what Gary was saying. It wasn't that Steve necessarily had blood lust; it was more accurate to say that Steve saw the falcons for what they were—compact, efficient killing machines. And I think Steve saw his role as the supreme facilitator, the master manipulator, the man who could make it all happen for his birds. So, yeah, he doesn't feel right if he hasn't killed something—or more accurately, if his birds haven't killed something—on a day he goes out hunting because, after all, that's what it's all about. He's helping the falcons fulfill their destinies.

By December, Steve's cabin quiets down. Most of the visitors like to come in October and through part of November when the daytime air is cool and crisp in the morning, warm in the afternoon, then downright cold at night. It's a party feeling at the cabin: morning hawking, followed by fishing or sitting and taking in the afternoon sun in the lawn chairs set up by the back door, and then an evening of drinking whiskey and wine and eating good food. By December, though, the hawking takes a more serious turn. It's much colder in the high desert, and there can be quite a bit of snow on the ground in the fields where Steve likes to fly his birds. With a change in the weather, the sage grouse gather in large mixed groups on the wintering grounds, and the easy pickings of early autumn are over. These are seasoned birds who have survived eagles and hawks and everything else that has tried to catch them, and they've learned to be wary of things in their world that seem out of the ordinary. It's hard to hawk sage grouse once the snow falls and the birds go to their wintering grounds. In addition to having wary prey, a winter morning of hawking can be cold, uncomfortable, unpredictable, and even precarious. This is the kind of hawking Steve likes best because it has an edge to it and takes more skill on the part of the dogs, the falconer, and the falcons.

Dave Cherry, the falconer from Southern California, came to visit Steve and fly birds during the first week in December. Cherry is one of those legendary falconers who have dedicated their time and energy to the sport. He's the one who wouldn't accept any compliments for the flight of his bird when it hadn't made a clean kill during the NAFA meet in Kearney, Nebraska, which had been just a week or two earlier. He's as hard core as they come and, consequently, Steve really enjoys Dave Cherry's company.

On the first day of hawking, and after some great flights with their birds, each falconer walked out of the field with a grouse in hand. Steve was feeling particularly good because when he'd flown Zaduke late that morning, the young hybrid had caught his first wild mallard, flushed from some open water that was fed by a warm spring.

This young bird was one I had seen fly earlier in the season. Although Steve really wants his birds to fly on just sage grouse, he often trains them using bagged ducks. When I was at the cabin in October, Steve was worried about the lack of aggression in Zaduke. "I'm worried because he doesn't seem to have that killer instinct, so I don't know if he'll ever be a good bird," he said. He spent a fortune buying mallards from the game farm and then throwing them in the field for Zaduke, day after day. On the day I saw him fly, he went pretty high in the sky, but when Steve released a bagged mallard, the falcon put in a half-hearted stoop on the duck as it flew fast and low toward what it hoped would be the safety of some distant hills. Steve called the falcon down by throwing the carcass of a dead sage grouse high into the air and then watched as the falcon came down on the dead bird. "Jesus, how many ducks do I have to buy and then just throw away?" Steve said as he picked up Zaduke, hooded him, and put him in the back of the truck. At twenty dollars a duck, Steve felt like he was just throwing money away—basically providing eagle food as the farm-raised ducks searched for water in unfamiliar surroundings. We'd gotten into the truck and then bumped along on the two-track, neither of us speaking while the radio blared songs about trucks and women and long-lost loves.

The fact that Zaduke had caught a wild duck that December morning meant that the bird was finally making the connection, that he was figuring out what it meant to be a hunter. So Steve was feeling good about his birds and his life and his place in the world when he and Dave went hawking the next morning. It was a cold, crisp day; they had been out in the desert for quite a while and were on their way back from grouse hawking when they saw a small pond with several mallards on it. Steve decided to put Zaduke up. Although Zaduke had gotten some valuable experience by catching the wild mallard the day before, he was still inexperienced at flying wild ducks and didn't seem to know that if he didn't catch one right away, he couldn't catch one by chasing it. The ducks rose from the pond when Steve and Dave flushed them, and off they went with Zaduke in hot pursuit. Those ducks flew as hard as they could across the desert in search of some place to land where they would be safe from the falcon.

Steve and Dave jumped into the truck, and Steve rolled down his window and pointed his telemetry receiver out, hoping to track the signal from the transmitter attached to the falcon's leg. As he blasted across the snowy two-track, he kept changing the angle of the antennae—*beep beep beep*—and finally he picked up a weak signal and drove in the direction it was coming from. The signal got stronger as they neared a small bluff above the Big Sandy River. Steve had a feeling of dread when he saw an eagle circling above them. He got out of his truck and looked down toward the river. He saw all the ducks crowded into a little bit of water, and an eagle sitting on the icy bank holding Zaduke in his foot.

Steve began yelling and charged down over the face of the bluff. The eagle dropped the falcon and took off.

When Steve reached Zaduke, the falcon was dead. Steve looked at the scene and tried to reconstruct what had happened.

"There were a couple of mallard feathers on the snow and my bird looked a little bit wet," Steve told me later. "He was a real rookie and I had been giving him bagged ducks out in the sagebrush so he thought he could just go in and grab a duck from the water. The water wasn't very deep, but when my bird tried to grab the duck, he got all wet and most likely ran over onto the side of the bank. The eagle was probably watching all this and was able to get him right there because Zaduke was wet from being in the water, which made it harder for him to get away."

That was on a Tuesday morning, and by the time Steve got back to the cabin he felt terrible. All the way home he'd kept thinking about what must have happened—about the mistakes he might have made in the falcon's training and the mistakes the bird had made out in the field. Although Steve was thankful it wasn't one of his other birds, it was sickening to have a dead falcon in the back of the truck. He thought about all the bagged mallards he had thrown for the first-year bird, about the hours and hours that had gone into teaching the bird to develop a taste for the hunt. And all of a sudden, he was back to square one: his bird was gone and he'd have to start all over with a new bird. By the time Dave left that afternoon, Steve was pretty depressed.

But he didn't have much time to feel sorry for himself because another falconer from Colorado was arriving at the cabin later that day. This was a guy Steve had met at the NAFA meet who wanted to breed his dog to Tucker. He had called a few days earlier and said his dog was in heat, so Steve had told him to come on over. But when the two dogs got together that evening, Tucker didn't seem interested in the female dog, and Steve told the guy that he had waited too long and his dog was no longer in heat. Even though he was feeling depressed about Zaduke and wanted nothing more than to be alone, he felt bad that the man had driven all the way from Colorado for nothing, so he asked him if he wanted to go out early the following morning to watch Steve's falcons fly.

When they got into the field the next morning, Steve decided not to fly Jomo because he saw only big cock birds. He knew Jomo wouldn't attempt to kill a big bird, and he didn't want his old bird to feel frustrated. He decided to fly Jahanna, his four-year-old hybrid, so he put the transmitters on him for the early-morning flight.

As they neared the field Steve wanted to fly in, they saw an eagle sitting on a rock. The man from Colorado pointed to it and said, "Aren't you worried about that eagle out there?" Steve told him that he wasn't too concerned because the sun hadn't even poked up over the horizon yet. He explained that these big birds had their routines and usually wouldn't hunt that early in the morning.

This was certainly true of the eagles that lived in the area. But what Steve didn't know was that the recent cold front had brought migrating golden eagles in, and they were likely to be hungry and looking for any opportunity to get food.

Steve drove along a little ridge and then up to the place he called Avalanche Hill—where years ago his truck had slid down off the ridge—and then up onto a large flat area. As they drove along, a huge flock of grouse lifted off the snow-covered desert. Steve knew a dozen or so would still be hiding behind the sagebrush. The eagle they had seen was in the canyon to the left of where they were flying. He stopped the truck, let Tucker out, and put Jahanna up.

Jahanna was turning out to be an amazing falconry bird. He was fearless and fast—when he got a grouse beneath him, he would not let it get away and hurtled toward earth at a speed that was breathtaking to witness. Once, when Tim and I were visiting Steve, Tim had been amazed when he'd seen Jahanna fly. "That bird is fabulous," he'd said as Jahanna folded his wings and dropped toward the earth from a thousand feet up. Here was a bird that was going to be one of the great ones in the line that stretched from BBG to Smokey to Kallikak to Jomo. Jahanna had the potential to be the next Jomo. If Jahanna continued to fly as well as he had been that season, he could be the bird that would take Steve through old age.

That morning Jahanna flew really high. The bird ringed up above the falconers, and because the falcon had gone so high, the guy from Colorado asked Steve if he ballooned his birds. (Ballooning is often used when falconers don't have big fields to fly their birds in; Steve never balloons his birds because he has all that wide-open space available.) Tucker was running downwind about a hundred yards ahead of Steve when suddenly a hen grouse burst from the cover in front of the dog. Jahanna was so high that he came streaking across the sky and, after a spectacular stoop, hit the grouse with a *whack!* He then flew back up several hundred feet while the grouse bounced off the ground, recovered, and took off for the canyon with Jahanna right behind her.

When Steve and the other falconer saw what was happening, they ran the couple of hundred yards back to the two-track, where the trucks were parked. *Ka-thump ka-thump ka-thump*—Steve's heart was working overtime as he got in the truck. He fumbled to get the receiver antenna open as he headed in the direction of the canyon, driving with one hand and holding the antenna out the window with the other. He got a really strong signal when he pointed it down to the canyon. Then suddenly the signal changed and it sounded like the bird was coming close to him: *beep beep BEEP BEEP BEEP.*

That's when he saw the eagle flying up the canyon.

Steve threw the receiver on the seat next to him and began honking his horn and driving as fast as he could toward the eagle. *REEE REEE REEE.* He just laid his arm across the horn—*REEEEEEEEEEE*—and the eagle, a big female golden eagle, came blasting out of the canyon and flew right over the truck. Jahanna was flying ahead of the eagle, but Steve could see that something was wrong because Jahanna was not flying at full power.

REEEEE REEEEE. Steve floored the truck and followed the birds. The dusting of snow on the desert floor blew up like a cloud of fine powder behind the truck. Forty miles per hour. Forty-five miles per hour. The Toyota was almost airborne as it went across the desert floor plowing over sagebrush bushes in its path.

The eagle was closing in on Jahanna when the falcon suddenly flipped onto his back and put his feet out—a defensive move meant to scare off an attacker. The eagle grabbed him with her powerful feet and went to the ground carrying Jahanna, landing about a hundred yards in front of Steve.

Steve threw the truck into park, flew out the door, and ran full speed toward the birds. *"Ahhhhhhh!"* Steve screamed as he ran. The eagle got scared and flew off.

When Steve got to Jahanna, the bird was gasping for breath. Steve bent down. Jahanna stared at him with his big black eyes, and then it was over.

Steve picked him up.

In less than twenty-four hours, two of Steve's most promising birds had been killed. A few months earlier, he had told me what an incredible bird Jahanna was—that the bird "had a lot of heart in him"—and he had described Jahanna's recent performance at the Utah sky trials. "He not only flew the highest of any falcon but was right overhead after he stooped and hit his pigeon," he said. "Like a good showman, he rang up straight into the sky high above the crowd—what a good bird."

On December 6, the day Jahanna was killed, the falconer from Colorado wrote in the cabin guest book: *Steve—I hope someday we can breed some pups from Tucker and Gracie. I just hope that somehow that will ease the loss we witnessed today. I'm truly sorry—he was such a nice bird. Thank you for your hospitality. Come back strong.*

Jahanna's death was absolutely devastating to Steve. He loves his birds the way intense dog people love their dogs or horse people love their horses. "All of us have an emotional attachment to the creatures we care for," he said. "You get to where you love them." But it was more than that. Here was Jomo's heir apparent—and Steve's future—and seeing all that potential wasted because of a bad decision on his part was almost too much to bear.

He left the cabin the next day and went home to Salt Lake City, taking his remaining birds and his dogs with him. Over the next couple of weeks he took Jomo and Tava duck hunting in Malad, Idaho. After sage grouse, the mallards were really easy for the birds to catch, and every time the falcons flew on the ducks they were pretty much guaranteed a kill. And in true Steve fashion, he said, "It's still fun to hunt, but it's like sports. If every time you go into a game you know that you're so much better than your opponent, it's going to take away some of your edge. You know you're not pushing the limits."

Steve believes that if you don't learn something from each season of flying birds then you're doing something wrong. "That's one thing about falconry," he said. "You can become proficient at it, but by the time you really have a handle on it, old age is probably taking its toll on you and you can't do it the way it needs to be done. I've been doing it since I was a young kid and got King Frederick's book and tried to emulate the pictures I saw—you know, some kids go out and try to build huts and such and I was trying to build mews."

Months later, when he was able to talk about those horrible couple of days in December, he said he'd learned from this experience. He learned that he had to be really careful when the eagles were migrating through, and he was never going to fly his birds when he saw an eagle nearby. He just didn't want to chance it. He decided that if he saw an eagle, he would go to another area to fly. "You can't prevent it from happening," he said. "But at least you can reduce the number of times it happens."

I know Steve meant this when he said it, but I wonder if he

can stand seeing a dog on point and knowing there's at least one grouse crouched in front of it and not put a bird up, even if there is an eagle nearby. I'm not saying he's reckless or will intentionally put his birds in harm's way. I'm saying he may not be able to control himself. The desire to have his bird nail a grouse may trump reason. Steve loves all his birds, and presumably he learned a lesson each time a beloved bird was killed. But it has happened again and again.

Joe Harmer has probably spent more time than anyone else hawking with Steve. Steve's falconry journal entries are filled with notes about hunting with Joe. Joe's a cranky old cuss with politics to the right of Attila the Hun, but he's a good falconer and a good friend of Steve's. When Steve's at the cabin and no one else is around, Joe will come over for dinner. When Steve has people visiting, Joe makes himself scarce, because he doesn't suffer fools silently and so, before he knows it, he's in a political fight with the other guests.

Joe was with Steve when Steve had a bird killed in 1993. When they got to the flying field at Jack Morrow Creek in the Tri-Territories, it was late, around nine in the morning. They saw an eagle in a canyon. It was Joe's turn to fly his bird, but he declined because he had promised himself he'd never fly after 9:00 A.M. "You can fly," he said to Steve. "But I ain't." Steve put out a dog, and the dog went on point, so he put his falcon up. The grouse flushed and the bird tail chased it, and when Steve and Joe tracked the falcon down, it was sitting on a bush. Joe told Steve it was going to be a terrible flight. "Why are you doing this? Do you just want to kill something?" Joe asked him. Steve spooked the falcon off the bush, and soon it disappeared down Jack Morrow Canyon with the men running after it.

"I went up on the ridge to try to get better reception from the receiver and I seen Steve walking back through the sage toward the road and both hands are down and I knew the bird was killed," said Joe. In Steve's game bag was his white gyrfalcon without a puncture wound or a drop of blood on it. "It literally had the life squeezed out of it—the eagle's talons went completely around it," said Joe.

"You don't want to be with him when he gets a bird killed," said Joe. "He relives that over and over. I haven't had a bird killed since 1983. There's only one way to cut that down—I don't fly in the morning anymore and only go out about an hour before dark. I can't push the envelope. If I don't get a flight in, there's nothing I can do about it because it's getting dark. By the time I go out probably ninety percent of the eagles have eaten, but in the morning none of them have eaten and they're all looking for something. When you was allowed to take three grouse a day, I would go out in the morning and then again in the afternoon because I was really greedy. But now you can only have one. As long as they're going to let me have any, then I'm going to be legal.

"Steve's careful," Joe said. "But he'll push the envelope a little bit and he took a chance when he lost Jahanna because he saw an eagle."

The last time I visited the cabin in Wyoming, it was the summer after the two falcons were killed by eagles. I went inside and entered the narrow hall and walked through what I thought of as the gauntlet of legendary falconers who stare out from the Falconers' Wall of Fame. I went directly to the stone fireplace. There, on the mantel, taking their places in the shrine to fallen falcons, were framed photographs of Zaduke and Jahanna. They joined some of the great falcons—BBG, Smokey, Kallikak, and Rocky—who had passed through Steve's life and now sat silently in the midst of birds that had been killed by electrical poles, great horned owls, and golden eagles. These birds spanned four decades of Steve's life. The small snapshots showed the falcons doing what they did best—they were all photos of birds down on kills, often with outstretched wings jealously guarding the dead sage grouse in the clutch of their talons. And behind the photos stood a great big stuffed male sage grouse. As I scrutinized each photograph, I realized that the tableau on the mantel said it all—life, death, predator, prey, hope, despair, love, and hate. A sum total of a lifetime spent in falconry.

Epilogue

THE OTHER MORNING I walked along a narrow road on the edge of my village under the full light of the hunter's moon. The moon's light illuminated the road in a way I thought impossible because just days earlier I had taken my morning walk in pitch-darkness. Today I cast a shadow that preceded me and fell on the last remnants of asters and goldenrod that lined the road's edge. A great horned owl flushed from a low branch in a poplar tree when I walked past. I heard the rustle of the dry leaves as it pushed off the limb, and I stood and watched the silhouette of the huge bird as it took big, slow flaps of its wings and silently flew across the meadow, heading for the safety of the hedgerow several hundred yards away.

As I walked, I thought about what this exploration into falconry meant to me; thought about what I had learned by getting to know Steve and seeing him in action for so many months. As I'd spent the year watching hard-core falconers flying birds in the stark landscape of the high sagebrush desert of Wyoming and the gently undulating prairie land of Nebraska and the tight agricultural fields and meadows of upstate New York, I'd realized that I was destined to be a spectator of a sport that wasn't really a spectator sport. It's amazing to see a bird fly fast and hard in the field, but ultimately this is a sport for those who practice the sport, for those who understand all the nuances of the flight and the weather and the game and the terrain. I realized I was not a falconer and probably never would be a falconer, because the older I got, the less interested I was in watching anything die. It's that basic.

As I rounded the big bend in the road, the moon was low in the sky, directly in front of me, not far from the jaunty angle of Orion's Belt. I love this moon. It's the first full moon after the harvest moon and is called the hunter's moon because the light it throws is so bright that hunters can pursue their prey by it. Cirrostratus clouds covered half the sky, but the deep dark blue of early morning shone through the high wispy clouds, making the brightest stars seem even brighter. The first lines of the William Butler Yeats poem "The Second Coming" ran through my head:

> Turning and turning in the widening gyre
> The falcon cannot hear the falconer;
> Things fall apart; the center cannot hold;
> Mere anarchy is loosed upon the world,
> The blood-dimmed tide is loosed, and everywhere
> The ceremony of innocence is drowned;
> The best lack all conviction, while the worst
> Are full of passionate intensity.

I don't know why these words run through my head on a continuous loop lately. Maybe because they speak of the dichotomy between head and heart, between what we know and what we feel. Maybe it's something as simple as understanding the first image and envisioning the falconer losing control of his bird and knowing he's watching helplessly as it flies away. I think of Steve watching his red-tailed hawk Shoulders fly up and over the mountain when he was a little boy. I think of the anxiety all falconers must feel when their birds lift from their outstretched arms and head toward the heavens. Or maybe it's a reaction to seeing how quickly Wyoming is changing because of energy exploration and feeling as if things are out of whack—as if we're letting energy companies determine which species are expendable.

A deep melancholy accompanies me on my walk. I've discovered that there are similarities among falconers—at least among the hard-core practitioners of the sport. The ones I know are loners at heart who show a fanatic obsession with falconry. They live for those momentary highs when the bird is way up in the sky or hurtling toward earth in pursuit of prey. They remember the flights of all their birds with absolute clarity in an almost spooky way—a trait as disconcerting as a kid rattling off arcane baseball stats. Falconers yearn for other people to appreciate what they're doing. They want people to come out into the field and watch them fly their birds, yet it's not a sport conducive to any kind of participation by an outsider except for flushing game or driving the truck.

I wonder if there's a place for falconry in the modern world. To watch a falconer fly his bird is akin to watching time collapse. He hunts the same way his predecessors hunted millennia ago, and probably with the same intensity even though his pantry does not depend upon it.

Then there are the outside pressures put on falconry. As flying fields disappear to make way for housing developments, and as game becomes scarce because of environmental pressures, falconers are pushed farther and farther afield in search of quarry. Who knows what will happen to the sage grouse in Wyoming? Natural gas exploration, coal-bed methane extraction, drilling for oil, housing development, and the West Nile virus have certainly taken their toll on the grouse and other wildlife in the Green River and Powder River basins. It's unclear whether or not the grouse have reached the tipping point beyond which their local extirpation at least is assured. Steve is convinced the sage grouse population is in good shape, but others disagree. Perhaps when the game is gone or scarce many fal-

coners will give up the hunt and be satisfied with simply watching the spectacular flights of their falcons. But for some, like
Steve and Tim, falconry is all about hunting and having their
birds be successful in the field.

I don't know if a person can really understand falconry without being a falconer. In a way, it's like religion. Intellectually
someone can know the various beliefs and rituals associated
with a religion, but unless he has faith, he'll never really know
the religion. Until someone has flown a bird and had a kill, he
probably can't really know falconry. Until he's felt the adrenaline rush and seen the life-and-death moments, the knowledge
of falconry is academic. For the hard-core falconers, this kind
of knowing is in every fiber of their being.

Falconry is a lonely pursuit, but I don't think falconers are
lonely. They're too focused to be lonely. They're doing something that gives them enormous pleasure and enjoyment, and
for those of us left on the outside watching and waiting, there's
nothing we can do but accept it and be happy because they're
happy.

Yesterday morning I accompanied Tim to the field to watch
him fly his peregrine, Macduff. Rummaging around for the car
keys, I pulled a quarter out of my tan barn-jacket pocket. For
some reason I took a look at it and was shocked to see the profile of a peregrine on the back of the coin. *Ah, Idaho, that makes
sense*, I thought. This might mean the Peregrine Fund, which is
located in Boise, now has more political weight than the potato
farmers do.

It was cool and drizzling when we reached the field and
parked the Jeep. Tim brought his bird out from the back of the
vehicle, checked to make sure the telemetry receiver was working, then started walking down a dirt road that ran through a
hedgerow of hardwoods. I ran to catch up, then stood at the
edge of the open meadow while Tim took Macduff fifty yards
into the field. He reached over and loosened the braces of the

falcon's hood with his teeth and right hand and stood there with his left arm outstretched. The falcon shook his feathers, looked around, then pushed off from Tim's glove and began a slow ascent into the leaden sky.

Tim still uses bells on his bird, something Steve won't do because he doesn't want golden eagles to hear his bird when it's flying. But in the East, where the fields are small and hemmed in by trees, Tim wants to hear where his bird is at all times. *Ching ching ching ching.* The sound of the bells attached to the bird's ankles was comforting as Macduff began to ring up. As Tim ran to the little pond on the field's edge to flush some ducks for his bird, I stood back, closed my eyes, and felt the rain on my face as I listened to the falcon's bells high above my head.

Acknowledgments

WHEN I MARRIED Tim Gallagher in 1991, I didn't realize I was also entering into the world of falconry. I couldn't even tell a robin from a blue jay—much less a red-tailed hawk from a peregrine falcon—so when that little kestrel ended up on Tim's desk at work and Tim's falconry was awakened, it was a shock. Over time, as Tim became more immersed in his sport, I realized I wanted to know a lot more about this quirky little subculture. I mean, who were these people and why did they want to hunt with birds of prey? Meeting falconers and then watching them fly their birds at the New York State Falconry Association meets in Cortland, New York, and the North American Falconers' Association meet in Kearney, Nebraska, was wonderful and it really did make me want to know more.

Without the cooperation and friendship of Steve Chindgren and his family, I could not have written this book. I am extremely grateful to them for their patience and their hospitality as I asked them countless questions and intruded upon their daily lives. Steve was enormously generous in letting me stay at his cabin in Wyoming for weeks and I came to love the starkness of that high desert landscape. I would like to thank my agent, Russell Galen, for sticking with me and helping me to figure out what this book was really about. I am particularly grateful to my editor at Houghton Mifflin Harcourt, Lisa White, who made the final product much better.

Several people read all or part of the manuscript along the way—my mother, Jane Dickinson; Mary Woodsen; Bobbi Dempsey; Kristin Ohlson; Jane Boursaw; Pam Oldham; Gwen Moran; Jenna Schnuer; and Kathleen Conroy—and I would like to thank them for their honest appraisals.

Finally, without the help, support, and love of my family— Tim Gallagher, Railey Savage, Clara Gallagher, Jack Gallagher, and Gwendolyn Gallagher—I would be nowhere.